LEVERAGE

Ron Rapatalo

Thought Leader Press

Contents

Introduction

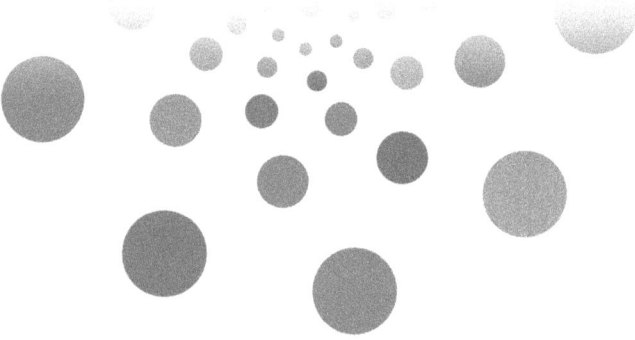

"Why me?" is a question I'd like to ask right at the start.

I think I've learned in my adult life, between the ages of 0 to about 47, that you don't just get a job because you're smart, and it's solely about your talent.

I think I learned over time, even in grade school, that it was about the people I surrounded myself with. The whole idea of leveraging the people who love and care about me, personally and professionally, accentuated the foundation of my talent and provided me with the resources.

Lessons from Mr. Seluga in fifth grade and Mr. Irgang in high school, the many people in college and student life who influenced me, and my taste for student leadership and activism helped me to understand that when you leverage people to do something, it gets you a lot farther.

At first, I didn't take a lot of the lessons I had learned from college into the workplace.

I decided to bury my head in the sand. I said to myself, 'Ron, just work really hard. People will notice you, and it'll, all be figured out when you have the performance review, just like when you get a hundred on a test and they give you an A grade because you did well.'

Unfortunately, that is different from how the workplace functions, and several harsh realities later I started figuring out that you can have a great performance review but it doesn't necessarily get you promoted.

I remember feeling resentment early in my career, and some of it was just because I was, and I still am, competitive. I was watching folks who were in their mid-20s or early 30s, already leading teams and starting to achieve a lot more than me.

I started to think, 'wait, how are these folks 'passing' me?' I started questioning my career, between wanting to go to medical school, deciding not to do it, then meandering through careers working in higher education and finance.

When I started working in education in the nonprofit sector and I started hiring people, I understood things differently. I started to realize – 'wait a second, oh, this is how you assess people to get in the door?'

I then started coaching people on what the process was because they were asking me questions like "you're the one interviewing, right? How do I get my shot?"

And I think over time, a confluence of things had me saying to myself, 'I'm giving people all this advice as the 'career therapist,' even when I didn't label myself as such. Even in my late 20s - early 30s, I started thinking, 'why am I not doing this for myself in the workplace?'

Eventually, it became this inflection point. I remember a moment when I had been at New Leaders, a nonprofit, for seven years, and I began to feel this resentment really come to a bubble. There was a meeting we had amongst our bigger team and my colleagues were getting promoted. And I remember thinking, 'wait, I'm still a senior manager? What the hell? I'm not a director yet? What the F?'

I remember just kind of feeling anger, then talking to my manager about it, and saying, "is it always like this?"

I was not one to usually speak up about these things, but this emotional boil was making me feel as though I was not being valued. She replied saying, "No, Ron! We do value you!" A couple of weeks later, I got promoted to director. It's funny how it all happened, isn't it?

There were people who obviously loved and cared about me professionally, but I didn't speak up for myself and leverage those relationships to comfort me. I did not talk to my manager, who I already had a good relationship with, and say, "we need a way around this, I want to do more, but I'm not seeing it in my title or in my pay." And that began my journey of understanding that I've always been good with people.

I've always had people who trusted me. I learned how to work hard from the very beginning thanks to my humble roots. Being Filipino-American, learning from my immigrant story and growing up around lots of different people gave me both a lived experience and professional experience.

I do executive searches for a living. I've been doing it since 2014 formally, but I've been involved in hiring since 2003, so I have 20 years of experience in hiring. I've been career coaching informally and formally since then too.

I have industry expertise, but then I also have the stories because of my identity and what I've learned from being Filipino-American. Growing up in New York City and working in multiple sectors like higher ed, finance, non-profits, school districts, and for-profit firms has shaped me into who I am.

I started to piece things together because of the confluence of experiences I've had and the people I've run into and developed relationships with. I think it provided me with a broader perspective on how you can leverage people who love and care about you personally and professionally.

One thing I've always learned to do, which I think is kind of imparted in this book, is I can almost imagine the beginning of a story. My beginning, like in any book is like, "let me tell you a little bit of a story about me, who I am, and how I got to this point."

Why would you care to read the content? It would just be some of this stuff that I think needs to be zoned in on. But I have all these lessons that I've learned from folks and, fast forward 20 years, I now have hiring experience at all levels, I'm supporting clients across the country and I'm coaching folks across all levels, from college students through to executives.

I think my sweet spot, really, is leadership. If I think about the zoning in this book and about who it's for, it is really for the leaders. Although I think anybody can read it, my professional expertise and most of the people who I tend to talk to are folks who are in the leadership seat.

What I've found, because I've watched many sectors, and particularly the sector that I'm supporting clients in, is that not every leader thinks about the social impact sector. Folks do the work and they're leveraging relationships, but not always for their career. They're leveraging their relationships for the good of the organization they are in and they're not always thinking 'what do I need to get me to where I need to go next?'

One of the things I often say, and I don't even think this is controversial because I tell this to people all the time, is that you should always think of yourself as a free agent.

Loyalty only goes so far. Having dealt with economic downturns here and there and been in organizations where they've had layoffs multiple times, my own company included, I've watched as we've had to make difficult decisions. I haven't been the one on the chopping block yet, thank God, but at the same time, I've watched when organizations make decisions like that.

I've seen that folks, at times, can have a myopic view of being so loyal to the organization that they're not thinking about their own career path and journey that doesn't necessarily have to fit inside where they currently work.

I had to learn that by accident. I got fired in 2012. I don't wish getting fired on anyone.

Getting fired was one of the biggest moments in my career and I sent out an email to 100+ people who loved and cared about me personally and professionally. I got an 85% response rate at least. Whilst not everybody was directly helping me by saying "here's a job," I received the emotional support of people getting on the phone saying "hey, let me see what you're looking for. Maybe I can help connect you to people."

In three weeks, I landed full-time consulting work. Three weeks is all it took.

We were in a different economic climate in 2012, mind you, but I almost got fired from another job in 2014 when I was consulting in a school district for two years. I was demoted and it seemed like I was going to be laid off.

I said to myself, with advice from my former manager who brought me into that school district, 'Ron, there's a playbook here. They've demoted you for a reason. They're trying to make you uncomfortable. They want you to leave. Leave on your own, or you might be laid off.'

I thought, 'what do you decide to do? It's your choice.'

Three weeks later, I gave in my notice.

The pattern is as follows: I've had folks just come in front of me where I always felt it in my spirit like, 'something bad is about to happen here.'

The first time I got fired, I didn't do anything about it because I felt shell-shocked. I remember walking into the office of my manager at the nonprofit in early January 2013 after the holidays to hear, "We decided this isn't working out. Here's your severance. You have to sign an NDA and all this stuff".

It was garbage. Two weeks. I didn't even think I could negotiate. I was thinking, 'I just had a daughter, I don't have a job anymore, what the F am I going to do? What should I tell my wife?' I just had to let go of all these emotions. I just took it and ran, thinking, 'I'm out of this place.'

That is the beginning of the story.

So what's in this book? There are these lessons and then there's the 'well—what did Ron do next?'

I really enjoy reading a lot of thought-leadership books, like James Clear's 'Atomic Habits'. At the end of the chapter I read: "Here are the takeaways. Here's the thing I want you to digest," and then each chapter has lessons like that.

In my chapters, I think there are lessons that I've learned over time about how I've seen the arc of building relationships with people through talking to a lot of people and some of the different career things that I've been a part of.

● ● ● ● ● ● ● ●

Talking to people who love what they do, that's one level of exploration.

Talking to people specifically about industries and jobs, that's a different conversation, right?

I want to help people understand where they can be learning and leveraging the people who love and care about them personally and professionally. When I think about the career advice I often give, I see it as being about gathering data from people and gathering resources and connections.

Another thing that I often think about in general terms is careers. It's a straight line, you can rely upon the people that love and care about you to probably get you your job, and those people's networks are what you need.

But if you're pivoting, I would liken it to if I went from executive search to underwater basket weaving. What a career shift, right? I don't think I have a network for that.

I'd have to do significant networking and rebranding if I haven't done it or if I didn't know the right people to get into that work, right?

I always tell folks, the angle of the pivot you're making for whatever's next will often determine the level of how broad your network has to start getting.

I like to just have a broad network. I know doctors, I know folks in Hollywood, I know lawyers, I know folks in government, I know folks in philanthropy, I know folks in ed, I know folks who are fitness trainers–I have this 'who's who' of people.

Now granted, a lot of that came from the privilege of the places I went to school like Stuyvesant High School, New York University, and different places I worked at and fellowships I've been in. I also worked into being part of networks where there have just been some ridiculously talented people who I still leverage today.

I was having this conversation with my wife in the car. She taught through Teach for America (TFA), the prestigious national organization focused on finding and nurturing leaders who commit to expanding opportunity for low-income students, beginning with at least two years teaching in a public school. I've worked there too.

The proportion of the people I worked with who went through two years of TFA are the most talented people I've ever met in the country. Social entrepreneurs, folks who've run districts, folks who've gone into nonprofits, folks who are running for office, such as Mike Johnston (TFA alum and former state senator) who is running for mayor of Denver.

One of the things I often think about is–when you surround yourself and build relationships with people, at some level your talent gets you far enough, but people pull you even farther.

I'm writing this book because I give this one-on-one advice all the time. There's a real selfish part of me that says, 'I just want this to be something where I can take all the advice I've been given, the stories and lessons I've learned which I've shared with folks one-on-one and in webinars. I want it to be something in print.'

I have four straight meetings today, from 10 to 2. And other days, I've been in meetings straight from 11 to 6. It's a gauntlet.

"Ron, how the hell do people like leaders have time to talk to people and help their career?"

Well, I'll embed it. Don't think that when I'm not doing business development and talking to people that I'm not thinking about what's next and what strengths I have and hearing about other people's stories.

Some of it is embedded in the way I do things. But I'm writing this book to put on paper, finally, the lessons, values, and mindsets that I've learned, to hopefully have other leaders start using those habits now.

When they decide to look around, they will see they already have the people in front of them who know what they're thinking, and they can excel in their careers a lot quicker.

●●•••••●●

I have found the job search disproportionate for leaders, and I know this because people contact me all the time saying, "Hey, Ron, I'm looking for my next thing."

They often tell me I'm one of the first people they are talking to. I ask people, "when are you looking for your next job?" Do you know what I generally hear? "I'm looking now, to leave in three or four months."

Do you know what harsh advice I give them in 2023? That might be really hard to activate. You know there's a hiring downturn? There are fewer jobs and there are a lot of people looking. Three to four months to look for a job might have been enough before, it was the case for me in 2012, 2014, and even 2018 when I started working full-time at Edgility.

But 2022, 2023? You generally need more lead time and that is based on finding people whom you can access quickly, that you have built relationships with, and who are willing to help you, give advice, and connect you to other jobs. Without that foundation, as a leader, it's like running a marathon and being 26.2 miles behind the race. It's just really hard to catch up.

So I'm going to zone in on one thing. I imagine this could be the pattern of a story, to teach and to show you how to spring to action.

I go back to what happened to me in 2012, early 2013 when I worked at that nonprofit. I got hired by them in December 2011. In January 2012, I was fired after five weeks. I thought I was doing a good job. I don't think I was reading the tea leaves that my manager was reading because of the way it ended up being.

Here's the action you need to take. Who are the five to ten people that come to mind that you immediately want to cultivate?

For me, it's about thinking about who's on your top list of people who you're always going to be talking to. 'Always' might mean monthly or quarterly.

People have used terms like the circle of champions, trusted advisors, and circle of trust. These are your mentors. These are the folks who have your back, and if you call these folks or text them, their likelihood of responding to you in 24 hours or less because you need their help is 95 to 100%. This is your tribe, these are your people. I think we all need that. You need folks who just 'get you.'

Who are those people, and how do you start thinking about them?

I have someone from my NYU days who I've known for 30 years. Allen McFarlane is his name. He was someone who advised me, He worked in the career center at NYU way back in the day. He's someone who has given me career advice over the years, so any time I'm trying to think about what's next, I usually ask him for advice. I contact him at least every year.

So he's in my circle.

I would consider my wife to be part of my circle of champions. There's a lot of stuff around my career that I've always checked in with her about.

You need someone who just personally knows what you value. I think about people who have multiple angles in my life; they personally know me.

One thing I'd advise you to do when you're initially building your circle of champions is asking yourself, 'who am I going to pick?'

I often think of the idea that people should think 'broadly.' Personally, I consider all the dimensions I have.

It could be someone I went to high school with. It could be someone who I've worked with or I've seen and done things with. It could be my friend Matt Baddie. He's operating off somewhere and he's very well connected.

You are looking for someone who knows you well personally, someone who is very well-connected. It could be someone like a current or former manager or a mentor from a fellowship that I did. I have all these people in mind, and granted my own circle of champions is probably larger than seven, but I have tried to make this book bite-sized.

My own circle of champions is really probably around 30-40 people minimum because I've just talked to a lot of people. But I had to pick seven, I had to take my bigger list and really boil it down so that it includes people who deeply know me personally.

My wife. Someone that has known me through school. Someone from high school or college might bring things to the table. Someone who saw me early in my career that I just kept in touch with, and who has seen me grow because you also want someone with perspective. And then finally, I want someone I've gotten to know recently who's seen me do the work, it could be a peer.

If I think of another person in my circle of champions, it's my former colleague at Edgility, Kevin Bryant, because he's pushed my thinking in many ways. He's a No-Nonsense Nurturer. I'm a nurturer, but I'm not 'no-nonsense.'

I often think about people who are gonna provide me with a perspective that's different from mine. I'm thinking about what my style is, who I am, and being able to make sure there are people in my circle of champions who have enough to overlap with me, but who are also different enough that they're going to push my thinking. I don't want someone that's 90% like me in my circle of champions. I want someone with a real deep value. Kevin and I are very action-oriented and we look at the big picture, but he is much more thoughtful and deliberate than I am. I'm always wanting to move fast. Kevin will often say "slow down."

As I'm thinking about how I came up with my circle of champions, it really was dependent on having awareness of who would complement who I am.

Allen McFarlane was someone who was advising me on career stuff early in college and I learned a lot of lessons there. I learned the usual stuff of not being afraid to ask for a meeting or a call. It's about unlocking the natural propensity of others to be generous.

That's my through-line here with the circle of champions. Sometimes we can feel varying levels of shame asking for help even with people close to us, like 'is this above and beyond even my own wife?' Those kinds of questions go on in my head.

Some of the things you need to perfect are the audacity to ask for the conversation, the meeting, the call, the lunch, or the coffee, and then structuring the question or advice that you need. Then, after it is over, how do you show gratitude and follow on from it, what are the next steps?

When I think of building relationships with the circle of champions 101, it's all about making the ask, being in the convo, and what you want out of it. Then, it is about the step to gratitude.

If I'm on the other side and I'm Allen, I don't mind helping Ron but I have so many people coming at me that I don't reach out to all the people that seek my mentorship and advice. I tell folks as busy as I am, I only have so much cognitive power to rotate in my frontal cortex. Everyone has to fight for my attention.

So at some level, even when you're starting, you've got to fight for people's attention because they may have their own circle of champions, and they're doing their own thing. If you don't stop regularly and have structured time with folks, it's really easy for relationships to fall by the wayside.

You already have the skill set to do great work. What I'm telling you in this book is that without leveraging the people who love and care about you personally and professionally, you won't get as far as you could.

In this book are some practical lessons through things I've learned myself on the career front. There is also advice that I've given through my executive search practice and career coaching that will help you actualize the people who already love and care about you better to leverage the next part of your career.

This is not hard, but you have to build habits to enable you to do this.

And to the person who's really busy with work, ask yourself, 'how do I build this into my calendar and my habit structure so this becomes, in a year, a lot more on autopilot?'

If I think about the person I'm writing this for, this is for the person who has good relationships, but generally doesn't make time to have these conversations with those close to them.

I understand you do great work. You give to others all the time. You probably have these conversations with others and you're not giving to yourself right now.

You're at a point in your career where you have said, "I want what's next, but I haven't really talked about it with anyone. Even with my current manager, I can't talk to them about what's next because I don't want them to be afraid that I might not be here for another year, so I don't have any people that I reach out to talk about what's next, but I have all these relationships in front of me. Both in front of me now and in the past."

My goal is to help you activate those relationships to have these conversations.

I want this book, and this work, to be a legacy for my daughters. When they start thinking about what's next, I will tell them, "read daddy's book."

But, of course, I also want this to be a book that I'm giving to leaders so they don't have to make the same mistakes I made. It's really easy, in the rat race of leadership, to be super focused because the time demands are crazy–that happens to me as well.

I want to help you to shift your mindset about how to start making time in your career now, to leverage the people who love and care about you, both personally and professionally.

– Ron Rapatalo, March 2023

CHAPTER ONE

The Empathetic Teacher - Mr. Seluga & Mr. Irgang

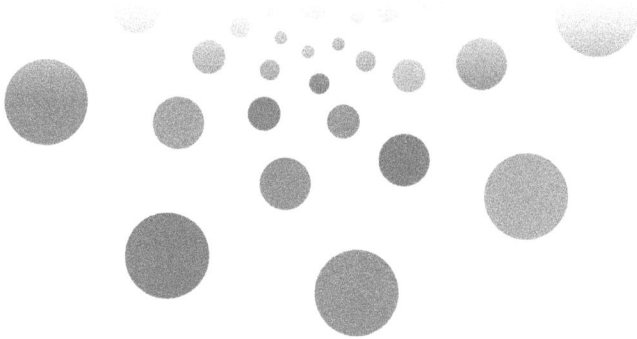

It was 1986, and I was in Mr. Seluga's fifth-grade class. I was 10, the youngest of seven in a Philippine immigrant family living in Queens, New York. We were a loud and rambunctious family who fought through many challenges. But at the end of it all, we had a deep camaraderie.

The Mets won the World Series that year. I remember an immense feeling in Queens in fifth grade. I was doing well and about to go to middle school. My father was going to take me fishing that summer.

I just remember a lot of great feelings like, 'yeah! The sun's out, we're playing in the backyard, hanging out, the family is working hard, and we're all in school doing our own thing.'

But then, on March 24th, 1986, my dad suddenly passed away due to a major heart attack.

It's one of those foundational moments entrenched in my mind. When it happened, we prayed like a good Roman Catholic family, and we all thought he would be fine. I thought he was going to snap out of it.

But then the lead ambulance said, "you know, we tried all we could, but he's dead." It was 3:56 AM. You know those movies where they show someone crying, and no sound comes out of their mouth? That's how I would describe how I felt.

As the youngest child, I was the apple of his eye. He was my superhero growing up. He couldn't do anything wrong in my eyes. You would have liked him if you had met him. He was like me – charismatic, hardworking, beloved, and really knew how to work the room.

Years later, I remember reading Brené Brown's Atlas of the Heart. I felt this intense grief and shock, shouting out, "God, why would you take my daddy away?" I had no idea what to do, and my soul felt like it had left with him.

I went through many rough moments after my dad passed, but the presence of Empathetic Teachers like Mr. Seluga, my favorite teacher in fifth grade, and Mr. Irgang, in high school, made all the difference. They became emotional anchors that helped me pick the pieces of my life back up after losing my dad.

● ● ● ... ● ●

The way my family and I coped with my dad's death was just like every family's shared experience of processing grief. It was rough. My mom literally collapsed and fell to the ground while watching my father being laid to rest. My brothers had to catch her. I was watching at that moment and to this day, I still can't cope every time I go to a funeral.

At the repast after my dad's funeral, I was struck by watching so many people showing intense love for my dad. Like, 'who are these people? I should be crying the hardest. Why are you crying so hard?' Then there were the stories about my father. His generosity, how hard he worked, how much he went out of his way for people, and the loving stories we shared about him.

A repast is a wake right after the funeral. It's the somber yet joyous celebration we had with my dad's passing. I remember everyone coming to our house. We lived at a corner on 123 Linden Boulevard, and it's funny because I juxtapose that memory with when my parents had their silver anniversary only 2 years earlier.

It was like these bookends of our house being filled with my parent's friends and family. A lot of people came to their silver wedding anniversary, then two-plus years later, they came to my house again to mourn dad's passing.

Of course, I found that, at a repast, you eat excellent food. Filipinos don't play around when it comes to a gathering – whether it is a death, birthday, or wedding, there's always a ton of food. This gathering was part of how we dealt with our loss. Being with close friends and family to share a laugh and stories about the good times with our dad was helpful. I remember having so much food to eat that it felt like we would have food for weeks.

After that, I remember a moment when my mom went into the basement, and I saw her quietly crying as she was sorting through Dad's belongings. I think you get back to life, and you realize all the little moments like, 'oh, dad's not in the corner office working right now. Oh, dad is not coming home with the newspaper so I can read the sports section. Oh, I don't hear dad trying to surprise my mom and mess around with her. Oh, that fishing trip isn't happening after all.'

As we tried to carry on with our day-to-day lives, the holidays were rough. It was like, 'oh, we're not getting

Christmas gifts from dad from now on and he's not going to bang pots and pans together with us,' which was something we always did at New Year's to celebrate. It was obnoxiously loud but it was part of our Philippine culture, and this tradition only amplified the silence of his absence.

35 years later, there's still rough moments. It's different now, though, because now I feel that he just hasn't been here physically. I believe spiritually, he's never left. But there are moments where I go, 'God, I wish folks could have met him.'

Mr. Seluga

I took a week off school when my dad passed. I remember the first day I returned to Queens, PS100. The teachers used to always bring us into the building and we all had to line up in a certain spot at the back of the schoolyard. Looking in from the street, we were on the left, back side.

I remember standing in line, and Mr. Seluga looked directly at me and said, "Ron, we're glad to have you back. I know you just went through a lot, but we see you. Is there anything I can do for you, or this class can do for you? We got you."

I remember that feeling of love. It hit me. I mean, I was obviously emotional about it. I cried when he told me that, and there was this feeling I had the whole year, even before my father passed as well as after my father passed, that Mr. Seluga really helped me dream big. That empathy of him seeing me gave me the comfort to both say to myself and hear, "Ron, what do you want to be?"

After my father passed, although I don't remember exactly when, he said to me, "do you realize you could be anything that you want? What do you want to be?" I remember him looking at me and I saw his blue eyes. He wore glasses, and he had blonde hair, which was starting to thin even then. He was a tall man, probably a good six feet or 6'2.

I remember him looking down at me and being like, "you do know that, right? You really could be anything." If I tie it together now, a lot of that was like Mr. Seluga being another father figure for me. I'm only thinking about that now as I write, it's the first time I'm really saying that.

At that moment, he became a surrogate father figure to me, offering support and belief in me the way he did. My dad had a special way of encouraging me, and I knew I could always go to him to share my good news anytime I got a hundred on a school test. My mom, after I showed her the perfect score, would nudge me in the ribs and say, "Ronald, go ahead and show your dad your hundred. He's going to be really proud of you."

Thinking back on that brings me back to my dad again. He would often be in the corner office of our living room just working. I would go, "Dad, Dad, Mommy told me to come to you, look what I did on my test." I would be beaming with pride and happiness and he was always quick to turn his attention away from his work to look at me. He would smile and reach into his wallet so that I could see his wad of money. I remember him always pulling out a bill and saying, "good job, Ronald." I remember feeling so happy having my father's love like that.

Another memorable moment I have with my dad is when I tried to trick him into giving me a dollar by creating a fake spelling test and pretending to write like a teacher, but I couldn't because my handwriting has never been very nice. I remember doing that and thinking, "Dad's going to give me a dollar." I think I wanted to go to the corner store and buy some candy bars. So I gave it to him, and he looked at me, smiled, and patted me on the head, like, 'nice try.' He didn't get angry at me. He clearly understood why I was doing it and didn't punish me but also didn't give me a dollar. My dad knew the intent of me creating the test was his show of appreciation and love. He knew to let my moment of kid trickery roll off his shoulder.

Having my father's approval meant a lot to me. So, after my Dad died, Mr. Seluga, as my first surrogate father figure, had a significant impact on me as well. That meant his approval meant a lot to me too.

Mr. Seluga was a protector. I was a nerdy fifth-grader and I was on track to apply for a magnet junior high school in Queens. One day during spring, I had an interview with folks from the junior high school and he prepped me up like, "Ron, are you excited about this? It's a really big opportunity for you!"

Then someone from the principal's office came out and said, "Ronald Rapatalo, please come downstairs for your interview." I remember all the kids were like, "oooh!"

I went downstairs to meet the interviewers, and the first thing they said to me was, "based on your last name, we thought you were Italian." But I was clearly Filipino, or at least clearly 'Asian-something,' because it was so visible from my eyes. That interview lasted maybe five minutes.

I don't remember what they asked. I don't remember what they did. I just remember being sent up pretty quickly. Mr. Seluga said, "you're back quick. What happened, Ron?" I told him what had happened. I probably remembered the questions they asked better back when I was 10.

I'm 47 now, I still don't know what the hell they asked me. Mr. Seluga turned beet red and said, "Ron, I want you to know that what they did was wrong. It was racist." I can feel it today, but I didn't have the language to process it back then.

I don't know what he did in response to that. I didn't ever go to that junior high school, but I remember the feeling of seeing that he saw an injustice happen. He saw me, and he was going to say something about it. Knowing that I, as a 10-year-old, didn't yet have the language or understanding yet to know exactly what had happened and why.

The interview had ended short, and I was thrown off. I was thinking, 'why would you think my last name was Italian? I've always been Filipino, why would you think I was Italian?' Mr. Seluga saw a racist incident happen to me. Because of the way I looked and how my last name was perceived, I wasn't given the time of day. That's what he saw. That's what I learned.

As an adult, having that protective influence has served as a guide to my own journey in the justice-related work I do to protect people today.

I remember in the movie, A Few Good Men, there is a moment where Private First-Class Downey looks at Lance Corporal Dawson and says, "What did we do wrong? What did we do wrong?" In the story, both of them were dishonorably discharged at the end of the movie. Dawson said, "We took a pledge to defend those who were too weak to fight like Santiago. That's what we did wrong."

I always go back to things like that because it's similar to a lot of the work I do when I see something wrong. Mr. Seluga saw what happened to me and tried to do something about it. That's what I do now. That's what I learned from him: to be a protector.

I leveraged what I learned from Mr. Seluga more as an older kid. I felt something was wrong with what they did to me that day, but I didn't have words to describe it when it happened back then. It was Mr. Seluga who taught me to start putting words to my feelings because he was just older and wiser.

It has been a long journey for me to learn how to access those words and be able to call out injustice when I feel something is wrong. I learned it's all about listening to other people's experiences, from people who are like me and those different from me.

It's also about educating myself. I read a lot of books and literature and the histories of people, including Howard Zinn's book, "A People's History of the United States." Reading the history of Asian Americans and the history of Filipino Americans helped me gain a deeper understanding of my own emotions and the context in which they exist.

In my line of work now as an adult, I constantly see the same injustices, both on an interpersonal and systemic level. What Mr. Seluga showed me that day was the importance of speaking out against injustice and the power of holding someone and saying, "I got you."

I like to give other people that similar feeling now. I like it when I can be there in the room, at that moment, to say to someone, "I got you." To be there in whatever way the person needs. Sometimes people say, "Ron, I don't need you to do anything, I just need you to hear me."

The lesson is that the Empathetic Teacher is around us all the time. You build empathy by being proximate to people who have different experiences than you and people you can learn from.

Mr. Seluga was one of those guiding lights and I am not the only one who had good experiences with him. Since he passed away, I have been in my PS100 Facebook group, and his name continues to bring up a lot of memories for people. He touched many lives as well as mine.

The people willing to teach us empathy are all around us, every day. To me, empathy is not just about having sympathy but actually understanding someone's experiences, even when they are different from our own. There is a lot to learn about how different people process their empathy.

Now as a grown-up, I have a lot of opportunities to have meaningful conversations with people whose experiences are different from mine. I tend to think about this from a racial and gender dynamic, however, identity is much more than that. There is a whole plethora of things involved and all kinds of domains to be considered. But for me, empathy comes down to believing people's stories. Mr. Seluga believed my stories. He didn't have to, but he did.

Asking questions to ensure you truly understand is essential, like, "this is what I think I heard, does that feel right?" This is a classic emotional intelligence technique and I'm not the first one to say this. This is something you can read about in Daniel Goleman's book.

I talk to people for a living and my lived experience of building empathy has meant that I get to learn people's stories. How do I learn their stories? I believe them first. That's my default.

We have a society that's built on not believing people. Society is often like, "that couldn't be your experience. There's no way." People say that because it doesn't align with their own experience so they discredit the story of others. But I do know that the folks who are the best experts on their lives are themselves.

If I could speak with him today, I'd say, "Thank you for seeing me, Mr. Seluga."

He saw me not just at the moment. He saw what I could be. He saw ahead.

I do the same for people now. I see ahead. And while I don't expect someone to see exactly what I see about them, I will tell them anyway. Clients now say, "damn, Ron, I haven't put that in words but I felt it. Thank you for validating that. You validated me."

As my clients tell me they feel seen, heard, and validated, I thank Mr. Seluga for this gift that I am now passing on.

Mr. Irgang

Mr. Irgang was a legendary teacher at Stuyvesant High School in the 90s despite his unkempt appearance and his hair that was a little bit all over the place.

He was an older white man. He had an untucked shirt half the time and an uneven tie. It was almost like having the Tasmanian Devil as your teacher. He was brilliant, and he was so animated.

Getting an Irgang recommendation at Stuyvesant was a real sign of validation. He wrote amazing college recommendations and described my friend Mark in high school like he was Superman. In these recommendations, we had to share stuff about ourselves, and whoever was writing the recommendation would write their summary of us.

I remember writing something about myself. I don't recall everything I wrote but I remember how Mr. Irgang used it. He said, "you know the best person to describe Ronald? I'll let Ron describe himself and hear his voice." It wasn't, "let me talk about Ron." Instead of speaking on my behalf, he believed in my ability to express my own qualities and strengths. He expressed confidence in how I described myself and would endorse it with his own signature.

I remember how I wrote that recommendation about myself with irrational confidence. I was around 17 or 18, and I was being irrational, although in a good way. I didn't know how the hell I was going to get places, but I believed things about myself like I was the best, the smartest, and the hardest working person.

During that time, part of me was wondering why Mr. Irgang didn't write me a Superman recommendation like the one he did for Mark and other people. I remember feeling a little bit off about this at first but after I processed it, I realized he was letting my voice come out. 'What I believe about myself is what he sees too.' This was the first time I thought about it this way.

Now, how well the recommendations worked for colleges is another story (I don't think I wrote good essays), but it didn't matter. I still got into NYU, which was my fifth choice back then because my mindset was Ivy League or bust. I feel a certain way about not being strategic about things like school choice. I would play the game but I didn't have money to access a college application writer or an essay reviewer and all these things.

But going to NYU was a blessing. 29 years later, going to NYU is one of the best things I have done in my life.

I landed where I needed to land, and Mr. Irgang taught me a valuable lesson by validating how I saw myself simply by letting my own voice shine through in the recommendation and affirming it.

Growing up, we didn't have a lot of money. My mom was working as a nurse's aide and losing my father's income meant that the glory days of having a $2.00 allowance weren't coming anymore.

At the end of junior and into my senior year in high school, I had a girlfriend. One time, we were having a high school prom. But, it had been so financially rough in my family that even doing something like going to the prom and asking my mom for money wasn't happening. I knew she didn't have it. I asked anyway and she said, "I don't have money for that. You have to figure it out. You got to work just like I did, Ron."

I remember my girlfriend being so excited to go to prom, and I was just ashamed. I made up all these excuses that had nothing to do with money. "I don't think we should go, blah blah blah." Word got around to people that I had no plans of going to the prom, including Mr. Irgang. He pulled me aside and said, "Ron if it would help you,

I'll pay for half your prom ticket. It's okay." I was so ashamed that I said no. But I knew he saw right through me.

Another special moment with Mr. Irgang was when he gave me a Philippine history book in his class. It was in a book closet that looked like an extension of himself. He pulled it out and said, "Ron, I got this, I want you to have it. A book of Philippine history. I thought this would mean something to you." It was so cool and I remember feeling that as he saw part of my identity, I should learn more about it.

I saw Mr. Irgang as a contributor when he offered to pay for half of my prom ticket. To me, it was the gesture of not allowing me to miss out on a foundational high school experience. He saw it as a moment for me to enjoy my young life.

Going back to those memories now as an adult, he was, in a way, similar, but also different, to Mr. Seluga. He was like, "I'm going to support you because I go hard for my students. I'll be hard on all of you. It's my way of protecting you all. It means that I have this really high bar, but I know that you can get there. I'm going to give you cover for your journey. I'm not going to just tell you something you want to hear, I'm going to give you a 75 or 79 on that paper if you deserve it and I'm going to give you feedback on how to make it better. And I'm going to make sure you get there."

Looking back, I was ready for that kind of treatment at that point in my life. I was ready to be accountable for my own actions. Mr. Seluga was a classic empath while Mr. Irgang used empathy in the form of tough love.

I wasn't that good of a writer, so I took Mr. Irgang's classes for two years. I was also irrationally confident that I started social studies a year ahead, which was not typical even for a nerdy school like Stuyvesant. They wanted folks to take social studies in grades 9 through 12, even though many of us took 9th-grade social studies in 8th grade.

But I was persistent, so I ended up getting credit for my 9th grade and starting in 10th-grade social studies. This meant I had to think about what I would do in my sophomore year and what I was going to do in 11th grade. I was like, 'well, balls to the wall, I'm going to take AP Microeconomics.'

Oh my God, was it over my head!

Being in Mr. Irgang's class was tough. His bar for writing and critical thinking was so high. As a kid who was so used to getting 100s and 97s and 98s on papers, getting 80s in his class was frustrating. I was like, 'what the fuck?'

I felt like I was on the struggle bus, but I found that my critical thinking and writing were also being sharpened.

I decided to go back for part two and I know Mr. Irgang saw me do that. Admittedly, I think it was also my irrational confidence that wanted to do the most rigorous thing when there was an opportunity. In Stuyvesant, being in Mr. Irgang's social studies and microeconomics class meant you were a smart motherfucker and a hard worker. I was a smart motherfucker who worked hard in high school. I wanted to signal that to people. Even though it was a struggle and it was difficult, I wanted to show folks I could do it.

The next year, I took AP American History. My writing was getting better and I got a 4 on the exam. I only got a 3 in AP Microeconomics so I didn't get credit anywhere for that, but I got a 4 in my American History exam. As my writing improved, I finally got some compliments. I was seeing less red markings on my pages when he gave me my essays back.

As someone raised to be a nerdy math and science kid, the beauty of Stuyvesant and taking Mr. Irgang's class was that it was the epitome of something that devloped my skills. I was taught that if you can't convey your thoughts, it will be hard for you to get by in life. Mr. Irgang also played a significant role in sharpening my verbal articulation.

Did they think Ron Rapatalo, a sophomore or a junior in high school, was ever going to write a book? At the time, I thought, 'I can't fucking hang with these people. These kids are giving all kinds of critical analysis and getting 97s on fucking papers. I'm not that fucking brilliant.'

I was intimidated until I became more confident. And it started with my second Empathetic Teacher, Mr. Irgang.

I started gaining confidence under his guidance. Even though he was setting the bar so high, he supported me all the way to get me where I needed to be. He saw I could do it, and I did, even though it was hard and I had to struggle.

Even though my irrational confidence initially pushed me in his direction, my persistence eventually grew into absolute confidence. I said to myself, 'Ron, you'll figure it out. If this is hard, then it's good for you.'

I have always liked doing things that people say they can't do because it might be too hard. I'm like, "No, it doesn't have to be." And that's thanks to what I learned from Mr. Irgang.

Empathetic Teachers

Empathy is putting yourself in someone else's shoes and understanding what they're going through. For Mr. Irgang and Mr. Seluga, empathy was about being able to truly listen and being willing to give feedback to people on how to get better.

One of the gifts we can give someone when we build a relationship with them is to say, "Hey, may I share something that I'm observing about you?" But that takes a certain kind of relationship. To share honest feedback with someone without trust as a foundation can easily tear apart any hope of building an empathetic connection.

Teaching is the easy part, but practicing empathy can be challenging. You can't teach without empathy. And while I wish people would automatically associate a teacher with empathy, not every teacher is empathetic.

But Mr. Seluga and Mr. Irgang were.

The critical lesson for me is that Empathetic Teachers are all around us.

I tend to put it on myself because not everyone will have the empathy I have. I don't expect it. And I can shift people's thinking in real time by being empathetic. We'll get to it when we get to the Manipulator later in this book. There are things I'm going to go through. I've learned a lot from the Manipulator; I did. I'm impartial to them, but I learned from them.

These lessons are around us if we're willing to listen to other people. It doesn't have to be an Empathetic Teacher. They're going to be a sliver of people in our lives. Mr. Irgang and Mr. Seluga were both notable, and I feel fortunate to have had them both as part of my life. But not everyone's experience is going to be like this.

This is why you need other people. Kevin Bryant is a No-Nonsense Nurturer who comes across differently. He is not an Empathetic Teacher. Ify Walker, the Visionary, is not an Empathetic Teacher either. My wife, on the other hand, is an Empathetic Teacher and a Personal Sage. While some people can possess multiple qualities, you can't expect someone to be all seven of the champions in this book.

I always put a lot of my effort where I have the most control – in how I show up. That's the lesson with the Empathetic Teacher for me. If I show up in the way that I want other people to see me, there is a likelihood that the lessons I have received from empathetic teaching will be around me all the time. However, some folks I've met do not appear as empathetic in their facade, but when you scratch the surface, you will find that they are. However, the master lesson I have learned is that I have to demonstrate empathy. A genuine demonstration of empathy changes people in real-time. You have to change the conditions by being empathetic yourself.

I was always working hard, trying, improving, and asking for feedback on how to get better. When I think of the father figures in my life like my dad, Mr. Irgang, and Mr. Seluga, they wanted to see that in me. They always asked, "are you willing to do the work? Are you willing to listen? Are you willing to improve?"

My unwavering work ethic earned me praise from these three influential men in my life. I knew that if I didn't put in the work, I would hear about it, and maybe in a not-so-kind way.

Folks often get focused on trying to find their Empathetic Teacher without thinking that it might be someone already in their life or someone that came to them with lessons in the past.

Someone can find an Empathetic Teacher if they're going through a storytelling process, like me writing this book. We may have encountered people who taught us empathy but didn't realize it at the time. We might not realize it until we start talking about our story.

Think about a time when someone listened to you and got you to feel at the end of the conversation that you learned a valuable lesson. What was that valuable lesson? How did that person listen to you? Were you surprised? Well, there's your Empathetic Teacher, and it could have even been your manager yesterday at work.

This book aims to show the power of leverage. You don't need to limit yourself to just seven people. You can have multiple Empathetic Teachers. These seven I talk about are just my archetypes. You may get to a certain point in your life where you might need ten of these and still might not be ready for the Visionary.

If I think about these things fluidly, these are the archetypes of people I've leveraged at different stages of my journey, and I wouldn't have been ready for certain people depending on where I was in my life. It's the honest truth. We are all different. There might be some people who are ready for all seven archetypes from the get-go, but I am not that person. All I know is that these people had shown up at points in my life when I was ready to receive them. That much, I know.

Everyone has a lesson to teach us if we show up to an interaction believing who we are and showing that we care.

There are three questions that I love asking when I first meet someone on my team at Edgility (I learned this from my friend Benny Vasquez): What's your story? What are you bringing into this space? What do you need? Because these are not typically asked, asking them offers a teachable moment. Learning to ask good questions, being curious, and believing people are all crucial.

It's like the improv lesson of using "yes, and." For example, "I heard you say this - and?" It's about diving deeper. There are often valuable lessons we can learn from this approach. I continue to learn daily through conversations with the people I work with or from simply bumping into someone in Starbucks. These lessons are around me all the time.

My Parents' Impact

My mom was the ultimate protector but my dad protected us in a different way. He gave provisions and made sure we had food to eat. But also, Dad protected us the way that I think I now protect people by default. Like him, I am the life of the party. I'm charismatic, I love forming connections and I love giving people advice.

If I think of the archetype of folks in the circle of champions, my mom is the No-Nonsense Nurturer, driven by working hard, getting things done and not putting up with bullshit excuses. Get up early and get the job done if you need to. Just get it done. That's what she learned from growing up in the Philippines and from her own life story.

My dad was the same, in a way. He was the youngest of his family and I think they manifested working hard for the "American dream" in slightly different ways, but the overlap between the two of them was the idea of working hard.

I would be remiss if I didn't talk about how my mom and dad loved laughing and having fun. I remember my mom would hide behind the front door and have me open the door so that when my dad came home, she would literally jump on him and surprise him. They'd laugh and share a kiss. I had very loving parents. It wasn't just about working hard for them. If you don't have love and joy, then fuck working hard. If you've got no love, it's like being dead. There is no hard work without love.

Becoming an Empathetic Teacher

It's important for us to not only be shaped by Empathetic Teachers, but to become them. That's the way we make the world a better place.

Here are three quick ways to become an Empathetic Teacher.

First, listen to people's stories and ask questions.

You need to believe other people's stories. Start by asking questions so you can truly get to know them and don't be afraid to ask follow-up questions to deepen your understanding of them.

Ask them who they think they are, what they're bringing to the space and the conversation, and what they need. That third question is the big thing because we're not often asked what we need. It throws a lot of people off to be asked what they need because many people haven't been asked that before. At least half the people I've asked that question had this initial reaction like, "I haven't thought about that. People don't ask me what I need." This simple question can help to build trust and deeper connections.

Second, believe in yourself. Have confidence in who you are. Answer those same questions above for yourself and be willing to listen to how others see you, based on who you think you are. In math speak, think of it like there is a gap between how you see yourself and how others see you. You're never going to get incorporated as one because it is asymptotic, but you can persistently try to close the distance.

Believing in yourself is classic advice, it's like something that Tony Robbins would say. It is about building your self-awareness and understanding what you're good at and what you're not good at, what you don't like doing and what you're passionate about. When you start articulating those things and write them down, you paint a picture and it gives you clarity of vision. So, then you slowly start believing in yourself.

Some people go, "Well, Ron, I think I could do X, but I don't really believe it." I'm like, "well, let's get practical here. Start with listing these things. You might not be there today, but how do you build up to it?"

And you can't start with it until you articulate these really practical things.

Third, and finally, teach others. Don't keep your stories and lessons to yourself. When you build trust in others, you can start sharing more of what you see with other people.

In professional performance management rubrics, this is about giving and receiving feedback. If you don't learn how to receive feedback, it will be hard for you to give. I'm starting in this order because for me, learning how to receive it for myself has allowed me to give it better. Sharing with others is like Empathy 201. It's the third lesson because you can't be empathetic if you just keep it to yourself.

Empathy is a constant practice. If I only do it with people I love and care about then I'm not doing my job. It means that even for those who are homeless, I am not passing judgment on why they are there. That if I'm giving money to someone who I know is going to use it for drugs, maybe I make a flip decision and hope they spend that money I give them for something else. It's not my job to figure out how they spend it.

Or, I can also practice deeper empathies like, "Hey, you know what, can I give you food instead? Would you take that? I'm not going to give you cash but I'm going to buy you something. We're going to the store. I don't want to perpetuate your drug habit because I know you'll use the money to buy some fentanyl." They may say no, but that's how you live with empathy.

It's really easy to live with empathy and have empathy for people you know well. It's harder to have empathy for Kanye West. That's harder. I'm going to say something really crazy – Do you have empathy for Adolf Hitler? That's even harder, right? He did horrible, horrible things.

Dr. King cheated on Coretta Scott King, but he did a lot of great things. Do I have empathy for Dr. King? Of course I do.

From a 360° view, the lesson of the Empathetic Teachers is that we are all imperfect. You are not going to have empathy for anybody if you expect perfection. Empathy is being able to see the totality of someone's humanity. That's the point.

To begin your empathetic journey, start talking to the people within your proximity. Open yourself up and share to them who you really are and what you dream about being. Be vulnerable. I don't think we do that enough. Build a trusting relationship with people around you and see how you start gaining more and more confidence. This person could be your mom, your grandma, a spouse or a friend.

This journey is going to be challenging for you if you don't build relationships with trust as a foundation and sometimes, you have to be the first one to reach out so the cycle can begin. Empathetic Teachers come in many forms and they appear in your life when you're prepared to receive the lessons they come to give you.

●●•••●●

Thank you, mom, dad, and all my Empathetic Teachers for validating the greatness that I was afraid, at times, to manifest.

CHAPTER TWO

Career Yoda
– Allen McFarlane

You need a Career Yoda in your circle of champions.

A Career Yoda is someone who has amassed a mountain of wisdom, and they will use that to support you in your professional life.

They can train and advise you through their words of wisdom. Through their being. Often that happens through conversation. If they think you need to fight for your career, they can train you to fight.

A Career Yoda, at first, is very hands-on as they help to guide you but that will lessen over time until you need them again. And when you really need them, they are always there because they never forget.

Allen McFarlane, my Career Yoda, has never forgotten a birthday or a major milestone in my life. He's also nominated me for alumni awards at NYU. He just knows what I did there.

You need someone like Allen in your life-someone who can provide a steady, guiding, quiet force throughout your career.

Allen was a bigger part of my life when I was an undergraduate and when I was just starting out in my career, but he's still a dependable figure in my life right now.

You should go and find a technical expert who does career work to benefit your career. From my perspective, that's exactly what a Career Yoda is.

It could be someone in your career services office in college. If you don't know someone there, then strike up a relationship with someone in the office.

If you're later in life, you should pay the money for it and find a really good career coach. You should ask around for them, ask people who you know and trust who have used career coaches.

It's important to ask around because you will want to find someone who really is an expert. You need someone who has a depth of knowledge across sectors. Someone who follows the research on jobs, industries and companies. You will want to work with a career coach who is well connected with people across many industries.

The Career Yoda, in some ways, can train you just by getting you in front of the right people. Not everybody in the circle of champions can do that.

Make sure your career coach is not what I call a "one trick pony." Make sure they have a multitude of abilities. They need to not only be able to give you industry specific advice, but they should also know the right people and know when to zoom out and provide perspective.

A Career Yoda isn't someone who is just going to be a technical advisor to you. They'll also be someone who's going to be able to hold you when you're weak, which often happens in career arcs.

That's who Allen McFarlane was for me.

He worked in career services at NYU for at least 15 years. He led the office at some point, but he doesn't do that as his main job anymore.

Career Yodas like Allen are trained professionals who have gained wisdom from having advised thousands of people throughout their career journeys. He doesn't just help people during their undergraduate degree, he follows their journey well after that too.

That's one of the really cool things about my relationship with Allen. He started helping me during my undergrad years, he helped me decide whether or not to take a pre-med major, and he continued to use his experience to advise me through different careers whenever I asked for his guidance and perspective.

● ● ● ... ● ●

I remember the exact moment I met Allen in my undergrad years. It was my freshman year in fall 1993.

I met him when he was an assistant director at the career services office at NYU. I remember him being helpful and seemed to know everybody.

To this day, he just seems to know everybody. A man who is all about the people.

He's very easy to talk to, and he still remembers details about me, even from my undergrad years. I remember the first time I sat down with him, and he was very friendly and straightforward.

I got my first student worker job, looking at the old index cards with jobs, when he tapped me on the shoulder and said, "hey, nice to have you here in the office. Let me know if I can be helpful."

After that, I saw him at events throughout campus and I always recognized him as being that friendly face.

Eventually I thought, 'you know what, I need to sit down with him.' I was a pre-med in college, so I was one of those folks who thought I didn't need a career service. I used to think, 'I'm going to medical school. Do I need to go to that office? Isn't that the office for people who want to work at some big corporate firm?'

Sitting down and speaking with Allen helped me to realize why I was doing what I was doing in my undergraduate. He helped me unpack exactly why I was pursuing pre-med at that early point in my career.

After a while, I realized that my 'whys' weren't all that good and compelling. Allen's curiosity about me helped me to really think through why I was studying pre-med at that time. I was grateful for that first piece of guidance that I got from Allen.

●●•••●●

I can clearly remember an important meeting I had with Allen during the time when I was trying to figure out what to do after college.

I remember sitting on a soft lounge chair on the eighth floor of the library the day of the meeting. I was studying for my MCAT and I was just on autopilot. I was reading something about organic chemistry and doing some quizzes. It was summer and it was really hot.

I was probably a little bit more uncomfortable than I cared to admit because I was going to sit down for an important conversation with Allen. I went into his office and it felt colder than usual because of the air conditioning.

I remember him sitting down with a big smile and he gave me a big handshake. He told me to sit down and asked me what was going on.

I remember he asked me, "are you making the right decision?" He just kind of cut right through it.

I felt a little bit shocked, and also a bit embarrassed, that I'd be asked this question when I thought I had the answer to it.

He said, "The reason I'm asking that is because I've gotten to know you over the years, Ron, and I care about you. And I don't get the sense that this is where your heart's at right now."

It's funny because I didn't really have a clear answer for Allen. I was just doing what I thought I had to do at the time.

That conversation ended up with me confessing, "Allen, I'm doing this because I don't know what else to do if I don't go to medical school." It was the first real moment of realization. I thought, 'oh, wait a second, I'm about to confide in him that I'm doing this because I don't think I have another option.'

He looked me in the eye and said, "Ron, you know you have other options, right? I'm here to help you with that."

This helped spur me to think about what else I could do. I had my student worker job at NYU and he told me, "You know what? You should ask those folks, there might be something full-time for you."

Funnily enough, my manager was leaving at the time. She said, "Ron, I think you'd be perfect for the job."

Now, this wasn't 'the job,' but it was the first job. It ensured that I would continue to have income after college while I figured out what was next. And I got it through the connection I had with Allen.

It was like my first actual "job to get paid." It wasn't a job that I was passionate about, but it was the job right in front of me.

It was good for me to know I had that option. Otherwise, I would have ended up applying for medical school. Not to say I wouldn't have been a successful doctor, but I was just doing it because it was the path I was taught to have.

Allen taught me that I would always have other options and that I should go ahead and create them. That was the first moment I realized I could create.

I think he could see from my body language, as an undergrad, that I could do it. I was a smart kid, I was getting good grades. I'd talk about my student leadership or other things that I did on campus. I would sit down with him and I think he saw that I was talking about it in a way that wasn't effusive.

He knew to get to the straight chase with me then, with the facts, because we had built a good relationship.

Allen's got the memory of an elephant when it comes to remembering people's details. That's really not easy to do. In a big university like NYU, you're running across a lot of people, yet he seems to know everybody that has passed through in the last 40 years.

I've been around NYU for 29 years and he's been at NYU since the 1980s. He just seems to have this sharp memory, like, "I met you at this place, do you remember when I advised you on this job?"

It makes you feel like you're being seen and heard. That's really powerful. I don't meet a lot of people who have that kind of social memory.

● ● ● ... ● ● ●

A big part of Allen's gift as a Career Yoda is his ability to tie things together from other sectors and seeing patterns of behavior amongst people.

After three years at NYU, I remember he encouraged me to think about Morgan Stanley and going corporate. He said, "you know, it's the end of the dotcom era. You don't seem to be thriving here at NYU. It's just a place for you. We knew it was just a job to have a job. Maybe you want to try another sector?"

I was open to it. The very first question he asked me, that I now ask other people, was, "well, who do you know?" I said, "wait a second, my sister works at Morgan Stanley."

There you go, right?

He just seems to be up with the trends. He mentioned to me, "Hey, these big banks are hiring because they're competing with the other dotcoms. And look, you don't need to have a finance degree to work at these places."

I had that in my head for my whole undergrad. I was always thinking that I should use my sister to see if I could talk to someone and get a job there. About two months later, I got a job. I was working at Morgan Stanley.

I appreciated Allen's wisdom, his knowing of the trends. That's not something I usually expect from people I meet, but he just knows what's out there because he talks to so many people and he follows what's going on.

Another thing I appreciate about Allen is how he approaches things professionally. I learned that approach from him and eventually started to practice it in my role.

He asked me what I was good at and what I liked and didn't like to do. A lot of his professional approach was to ask enough questions to be able to ascertain patterns.

That approach is used by most good career coaches, but I think Allen is a true Career Yoda because he can move to advising people a lot quicker than most coaches.

As I got to know Allen, he only needed to ask me a couple of professional questions and then he would say, "you know, this is what I've heard" or, "you know, I saw this with someone I've talked to."

He's always had a bite. Because of the social memory he has and how many people he talks to, Allen's always been able to tie things together well.

At one stage in my career, I had been thinking about going on an entrepreneurial track when it came to recruiting and I really wanted to pursue it.

I was paid as a full-time employee but a lot of what I did felt very entrepreneurial because I was working for a small business and we were scaling.

I remember having lunch with Allen and getting his insight about it. I asked him, "Allen, what's your take on entrepreneurism and search firms?"

He's always said, "you know, Ron, the money could be good. You're a really strong recruiter. You just have to ask yourself how much you enjoy selling. That's going to be the difference."

I remember having a lot of trepidation about selling because I felt it was easy to sell a job to someone, but I thought it was a lot different asking someone, "hey, do you want to pay $75,000 for a contract?"

I was afraid of feeling the acute rejection that would come with failing to sell.

Allen told me, "Ron, remember that moment when you just stopped feeling some kind of way about getting rejected by an applicant who you really wanted to apply for a job?"

I replied, "yes."

Then, he asked me what that feeling was.

That feeling is a realization that people often do things that have nothing to do with you and you just can't take things personally. At the end of it all, someone may still decide that they want something different even if you put your best foot forward and provide good service.

In that moment, Allen made me realize that selling contracts was not that different to selling jobs. You put your best foot forward and then you have to let the result go. It's easier said than done, but I appreciated him pulling that wisdom nugget out for me.

● ● ● ● ● ● ●

When I think about it, Allen is someone who cares and remembers. He just doesn't forget. Yoda doesn't forget, right? Yoda as a character doesn't forget, and Allen doesn't forget.

As an undergrad, he could have just supported me and said, "you go to med school, do what you do and figure it out." But instead, he tied everything together for me.

That meant a lot to me. From the conversations I had with Allen, I felt that I could be safe in admitting what I didn't want to admit, which was that going to medical school wasn't something I really wanted to do.

The fact that Allen really cares about people is something that has stayed with me since my undergraduate days. It's why I still seek him out every now and then.

I don't see Allen as much these days. Luke doesn't see Yoda that often, but he sees him when he needs to.

With me, it's almost like the student has become a master himself, and the new master will talk to the old master when he needs a little bit of advice here and there.

Cutting To The Chase

I was at an inflection point during my time at Morgan Stanley — I call it my "quarter life crisis."

Allen and I sat down one day, like we always do, just to catch up. I was a corporate guy just sitting down to shoot the breeze.

He asked me how things are going at my work, "Remember that advice I gave you about the dotcom? How are things settling in? How are you doing?"

I told him things were fine, but he wanted to know more. He knew this was an entry, for me to say it was only okay.

I explained, "I've been here three years. I don't know if I'm moving up or if this is what I enjoy doing."

He reminded me about the time that he asked me if I really wanted to take pre-med, and asked if I'm passionate about my job now.

I shared, "oh, it's not really here, I'm just here. I just do the job. I could do this job in half a day, but I have to stay here all eight hours. I don't feel very passionate about it."

He asked me about my passions and said, "Ron, I've seen you really passionate about the leadership work that you did at NYU. All the "giving back" and social justice works. Have you thought about doing something like that for a career?"

I said, "Allen, does that even pay money?" At the time, I didn't think you could get paid for that kind of work.

He told me, "Well, it's not always about the money, but you can get a job doing these things."

We started brainstorming and spitballing and he asked me that same question he asked back when I was thinking about Morgan Stanley, "well, who do you know?"

Surprise, surprise, I knew a lot of people who worked at Teach for America. So I started reaching out to some friends, and fast forward, I got my first job working at a nonprofit in the summer of 2003.

Allen saved the day once again in what was intended to just be a catch-up conversation for us over lunch. It was him hearing how I felt about my job, knowing that for me to say that it was "okay" meant something was wrong. He knew that I had to get out of that job.

I was very grateful for that moment. A Career Yoda will always cut to the chase with you when they see you really need help.

Knowing and Understanding People

Allen connected me to some finance people before I began working at Morgan Stanley.

He knew people in the industry and he said, "let me make sure if this is right for you. Check out Morgan Stanley, but you should talk to a couple of people that I know, who are alums like you."

Thanks to Allen's connections, I got on the phone with some people and learned a little bit more about finance and working at Morgan Stanley. They were nice casual convos. The conversations were nothing terribly memorable, but they made me think, 'okay, finance is not the worst job on the planet.'

I remember some messages Allen sent me over the years. He always remembered my birthday, and he remembered what age I was too, like, "Happy 29th birthday." He must put it in some calendar or something to keep track of those things.

His messages often come with some kind of statement like, "you know I'm always here if you need to chat about career stuff. Let's catch up soon hopefully."

Just a little nugget, a little reminder.

I was always happy to hear from Allen. I hadn't really expected someone from my undergrad years, even people who I had built a relationship with, to text me on important days, and let me know that they were there to help me.

But that's what a Career Yoda does, not only do they know the right people but they take time to understand and care for people too.

Having Wisdom

Allen was one of a number of people I talked to when I was about to get fired in late 2011, early 2012. I talked to a lot of people because I was really emotional about it at the time.

I was frantic, "it's about to happen. What the hell should I do?"

He assured me, "Ron, first of all, remember back in your undergrad years? You always have options. Remember that first and foremost. And what else do you know about you, Ron? You know a lot of people like me. We've got your back on this no matter what happens."

Then he asked me what I wanted to do.

Allen used his wisdom to flip the script and get me to stop seeing that moment as a time of desperation, but as a moment of creation. I ended up getting fired from the job a week or two after I talked with him. But I remembered that advice of, "just keep trucking along. You've been through this enough, you're going to figure it out."

And I did figure it out. That's all he needed to tell me.

He said, "I've got you if you need people."

But I had been in touch with a number of people by the time I talked with him. I ended up getting a full year consulting job at a school district in New Jersey within about a week or two after that conversation.

I needed my Career Yoda when no hard advice could have helped me. Allen's wisdom helped change my mindset and gave me the confidence to figure things out by myself.

Being Professional

I met with Allen about a year after I started working at Teach for America. It was a busy time, I was managing a huge summer construction project.

We always seem to sit down for lunch to catch up. Once again, he asked me how I was doing. I was really pressed at the time and told him I was overwhelmed.

He said, "Okay, let's walk through what's making you feel overwhelmed." And he walked me through a process of asking, "how's your workload? How many hours are you working? What do you have going on? What have you talked to your manager about? What do you think you need to do to have the load lightened?"

After having that conversation, I thought what Allen did was really brilliant. He zoomed out and said, "is this a job you're excited to have? Do you like doing this kind of work?"

I admitted, "no, not at all."

Then he probed, "do you want to stay working in education?"

I said, "I do, I'm pretty passionate about this work."

So he went back to that same old question: "who do you know?"

I knew some people who used to work with me at TFA that worked at New Leaders. I reached out to a buddy who worked there and got an interview within a couple of weeks. The interview turned into an offer. About six weeks after this all happened, I started a new job.

What I appreciated about Allen at that moment was the level of professional advice he gave me. He helped me unpack what was happening at work in a way that he hadn't done before.

It helped me realize that when you're in the throes of work like that, it can be way too overwhelming. But he was brilliant enough to zoom out and say, "let's think about the totality of this. Are you really excited about this job right now?"

I don't think I would have had the brain space to even think about how I felt about my work if he didn't walk me through all that stuff. It would have felt too over-whelming.

The professional approach of a true Career Yoda can really help you find the perspective you need to figure things out in your work life.

Being Helpful

Years back, Allen nominated me for the Michael Parkes Distinguished Alumni Award at NYU. For me, there was something extra special about the award because it was named after someone I knew who perished during 9/11.

I'd always been a very involved alumni. He sent me a note about a month before the award ceremony that said, "hey Ron, I've nominated you for this award because I can't think of anyone who's as involved as you are and who gives back to the university as much as you do. Someone like Mike would be really proud of the legacy you've continued with his alumni work."

I don't do that kind of work because I want an award. I do it to serve as an alumni. So, there was something really cool about him seeing me and never forgetting the work that I'd done at NYU.

Fast forward to when Allen was the director of the Center for Multicultural Education Programming at NYU some years back. There was a 30th anniversary event for the program and he was asked to chair it.

He told me, "Ron, I can't imagine anyone else, you need to be involved in this. I need you to co-chair it, from the alumni perspective."

He just always kind of knew to connect these dots with the work that I've done.

A Career Yoda always takes notice of what you've done and helps you out when they can.

Finding Your Career Yoda

Before you go in search of your Career Yoda, take an inventory of what you do well and what you don't do well and what you're passionate about. Reflect on yourself.

You don't have to be sure about what you're looking for, but I think you can lead with your answers to those questions.

I think a really good career coach can help you to come up with the lanes that best suit you if you let them know who you are. There's all kinds of formal career assessments you can also take to help you do that too.

I'm not saying that these career quizzes or assessments are perfect, but they are a good way to generate some ideas.

I think the best thing to do when you're unsure, ultimately, is talk to people who love what they do and ask them questions about why they love what they do and why they're sure about what they do. You'll see patterns.

You can certainly learn from people who are unhappy in their jobs, but there's something stickier about the advice that comes from people who love what they do. It can help someone be more sure about what they want to do next.

You could ask a parent about their work. You could ask a professor, or a mentor. You could talk to a friend. Your job in speaking to people is to figure out how and why they have decided what they're excited about doing.

The goal is to start developing your own rubric for that based on what you've heard from other people. Create your own process from what you learn. Then you can start to find out what job you would really enjoy doing. Then, maybe you know someone who has that job. Are they hiring?

Narrow down some potential roles and sectors that you're interested in. Talk to people in those roles. Then figure out which ones you want to apply for.

Second, write up something that explains what you're looking for in your next career coach. It doesn't have to be perfect and you don't have to share it with anybody yet.

Third, you start reaching out to people who have used a career coach, and explain a little bit about what you're looking for, without being perfect about it.

You can crowdsource too. You can go on LinkedIn or Facebook and ask if anybody knows a really good career coach, then just name a couple of things about yourself. You could say that you're a professional who's worked in sector 'X' who may want to switch careers, or you could explain that you're someone who feels stuck.

Fourth, you have to then screen the folks you've talked to based on the criteria that you've thought about. You start to refine your career coach options based on the conversations you have with them. It's important to think about your budget too.

Every career coach works very differently. Decide if you want someone who has an approach that is "canned" or "trademarked," or someone like me who's going to ask you questions that lead to a more flexible approach.

Finally, you have to commit. Committing to the work means not only showing up to each session, but working with the coach to figure out what your homework is. Most of the work will happen outside the session.

● ● • • • ● ●

People come to me looking for a career coach quite a lot.

If I don't recommend myself, I do know a ton of other people, it just depends on what sector and what approach they need. A lot of times, I have found that someone's experience matters, like their lived experience.

There are coaches out there with very specific industry experience. I have a friend who worked in finance and was an entrepreneur, so she can coach people on those things.

Every coach says they can be helpful, but it's good to name a little bit about where you are and what you're thinking because you may not know what you're looking for until you speak with someone.

I used to always crowdsource through social media. Now you can Google stuff, but in my experience, a good career coach is probably not someone who is spending their time developing and paying for their website to show up early in the Google search results.

Just like finding a good hair stylist, finding a good career coach is all about word of mouth. You've really got to rely on word of mouth and social media can help amplify that obviously.

You can also text five people you know who were success-ful in their career. I bet at least one of them has used a career coach.

People don't tend to make a move unless they've had some kind of person bending their ear about these Ca-reer Yoda-isms.

Your career might change throughout the years, but your Career Yoda is a constant.

A Career Yoda can help you when you're a beginner, when you have no idea what you want to do, but they can also help you when you know exactly what you want to do. Maybe you just need a little bit of deep fine tuning?

The Career Yoda is there for the entire arc of your career because they're always going to have something wise to say, or know someone, that can help you on your journey. And they never forget all the things you've gone through.

They'll be able to provide a perspective that no one else really can.

I often try to think about what Allen did for me. My work is all about coming up with lanes for people. It's easier for people to think of lanes once they get there. It's kind of different if you're still exploring out loud.

I really try to help people think of lanes, of sectors, or people to talk to. It just helps orient their mind a lot so it's then easier to take actionable steps.

● ● ● ... ● ● ●

If you have no Career Yoda, you can still get lucky and find jobs. You can get lucky, but you're more likely to stumble into success, rather than having that straight line.

The negative effect of not having Career Yoda is that you take a couple of steps back here and there because you're not getting that wise push and those professional questions at the right time in your life.

We spend a lot of our waking hours at work and if a person doesn't get lucky, they end up finding jobs where they just work to get paid, rather than doing something impactful or fulfilling.

That can have a negative effect on a lot of things outside work. It affects their mental and spiritual health.

I'm not saying you need to love your job so much that you bring it home, but I do think there's a level to be found where you enjoy what you do and you love waking up and going to do it.

Without a Career Yoda you're going to have to depend on yourself to find that level. I think I'd still be looking for it if I didn't have Allen shift me earlier in my life.

Get a Career Yoda for eternal career wisdom.

●●•••••●●

Thank you, Allen, for seeing me in the Career Services Office when I was looking for a student worker job and looked clueless.

Thank you for the advice, the training and the connections over the years, as my own career needs have evolved and shifted.

And thank you for always caring and never forgetting the small details like my birthday.

CHAPTER THREE

The Manipulator

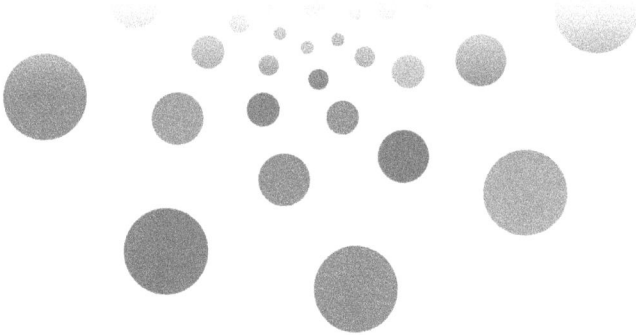

This is an important chapter and a really important topic.

Manipulators are willing to say and do the things that you're not always inclined to do. So let's see if there's a lesson to be taken from one of the Manipulators that I met along the way in my career.

Manipulators are willing to not be liked to get ahead. The Manipulator doesn't ever care about people liking them. I think there's something to learn from that.

They just get shit done. They think second about how other people feel, if at all. So there's something to be learned from that which I do take seriously. It's a balance to my natural orientation to want to "people please."

The composite of all Manipulators was one of my earlier managers. I don't want to name the person so I will be using the fictional name "Storm."

When I interviewed with Storm, the big thing I immediately learned from Storm was to be direct and to be vulnerable.

This interview was at a moment when I was not taking responsibility for my work situation in the job I had at the time. I think I was blaming my manager for things not happening in my career.

Storm just kept asking me questions like, "Ron, what's holding you back?" I told Storm, "I'm afraid, but I want to learn, and I don't know what I don't know." That was the moment of the interview when my vulnerability stuck and she thought, "I'm willing to work with that."

● ● ● ● ● ● ●

In our jobs, Storm and I, along with other team members,, had to travel to support other leaders and other program sites. I saw that Storm had this amazing ability to get people to like them. She was good at small talk, good at asking about the weather, good at knowing things about someone's family and all those types of things.

She has always been good at that. It's just their reputation. When I first met her, I thought, "oh, geez, they're really likable, they're really personable." They was good at getting to know details about their colleagues' personal lives.

The thing I learned from Storm is that good work is foundational, but it's just as foundational for people to like you.

People like you and trust you more when you can schmooze and get to know them. That often involves, at times, listening to personal things about someone's life. They was always good at getting that stuff out of people.

We'd travel places, and she'd take people out to lunch and out to coffee. There was a culture on our team, of us spending time together and getting to know each other. I think this is where the line got a little blurred with being friends with people versus being colleagues.

I do think that I've learned professionally, years and years later, that you have to be careful about those lines. If you're managing someone and if they're also friends, how do you hold them accountable? That's hard.

I'm not saying it's impossible, but I think that I watched that line really get blurred while working with them on these two different occasions. I saw this line get blurred with people she hung out with but also worked closely with. It could feel like those were the folks that she treated differently and in ways that were inequitable, versus others that she wasn't as close with.

Sometimes schmoozing gets in the way of being able to be an effective leader. That's what I also learned from watching Storm.

Some of this started at the first job that they managed me. One of the things I learned from her leadership style was that she had a clique, usually of other women, that she either managed or worked closely with whom she also built close relationships.

They hung out outside of work. They always had lunch or coffee together. They rarely pushed back on her leadership. When they tried, she shut them down.

I observed the transition, from realizing that there are really a lot of positives in schmoozing, and how the schmoozer can be a Manipulator.

There were people there that she was working closely with that I was also interacting with. It was almost like holding your breath when you see Storm walk into a room, like, "oh, she's here, we have to act differently now."

You had to act differently because you didn't know how you were going to get treated. Maybe something you said was going to be held against you because you didn't get along with Storm, or you did something that was against the way that they wanted the work to be done.

● ● ● ● ● ● ● ●

Fast forward to part two of my working relationship with Storm. I played a part in getting Storm to my new workplace and helped them through the process. They became my manager again, and I was excited about it because I generally remembered the warmer feelings I had from working with her rather than the negative ones.

Storm was personable and supportive. Storm knew a lot of people and seemed well respected. One of the things I realized about Storm in this newer context was that they liked working with specific people - people who would follow orders and not push back. But I found out pretty quickly that I was not one of them. In about six months, she said, "yeah, I don't think you know how to do this. I don't think you're the right fit for this role. I still want to keep you, but we need to bring you to another role."

I had never been told in any professional setting that I was going to get demoted. I was really thrown off.

I didn't know how to push back and advocate for myself. I thought, 'wait a second, how are you not supporting me to do this? You're expecting me to do this and yet you're not supporting...'

I didn't have the language to push back against the Manipulator and say, "You're saying I don't have the skillset, but have you given me the opportunity to do it?" My 'aha' moment came when I spoke with a former manager. I realized that Storm acted like this in other settings. She told me, "She is trying to get rid of you, Ron." That's when I knew in my bones that this was happening. It was a move from the HR playbook. If you demote someone and you start to make them feel uncomfortable, it's a way to have someone leave of their own volition.

It was like a laser from a gun was put on me and I was unsure if I would be shot. I know I had to get out of there. It was difficult.

There was someone new that was hired at that time, a 26-year-old who was kind of fresh in the workplace. I was told by this new person, who'd been there six weeks, that she was going to manage me. But I could tell that she was reading from a script. I interpreted that she was getting coached by Storm.

After being demoted, one of my primary new responsibilities was reorganizing Microsoft Office folders. I knew

I wasn't wanted at this workplace because I went from doing strategy and leadership work to doing administrative tasks.

It felt demeaning. It felt like they didn't want me there and they didn't think that I was capable of doing anything better.

I knew there was the Manipulator component within Storm, within the schmoozer. But at that moment it felt like I was in a movie when I fully realized that she was the villain all along.

I talked to my old manager, and she told me, "Ron, I'm going to help you." This was the manager who had first brought me into that workplace, who Storm had replaced when my old manager decided not to take a permanent role.

She said, "Ron, I love you. I'm going to give you this advice. They are trying to get rid of you. You need to find something else. Talk to the folks who used to work with you for help."

So I did. And I had six months of consulting work in three weeks.

Don't Care About Being Liked

For me, the fascinating part about not being liked is that it can be kind of a rallying cry at some point.

Storm's leadership style and the people she was closest with also tended to be people who were not generally liked in organizations.

It was almost like she got all the people who didn't care about being liked to band together because, "it's us against them."

They all had this style of, "I'm going to listen to your feedback but not doing anything with it because our way is the best way." They did that rather than say, "well, where's the middle ground here?" Or, "what's going to work for all of us to still get to the same goal?"

They didn't take the time to realize that there's wisdom in the crowd and wisdom amongst others. Instead, they said, "I have the wisdom, I'm going to tell you what I think is best, and I'm just here to convince you and I don't care if you like it or not."

That's destructive over time. We, as humans, don't respect that after a while because it starts to get into things like, "you don't respect my judgment."

People are smart, even if they're not conscious of the things happening at the moment.

The schmoozing got me to soften up, but then, the Manipulator came out.

It really came from Storm using schmoozing as a way to say, "we get along so well personally. I know stuff about you, but I'm going to use that to manipulate you because I really don't care if you like me or not. I use that to get you to do what I want you to do."

Be A Schmoozer

I started to get snippets of Storm going from schmoozer to more of the Manipulator when she made comments about the manager that had brought me into the organization.

Storm asked me what I thought about my old manager. It was really just gossip. It was like she was schmoozing with me to see which side I was on.

I remembered answering, "we have a great work relationship."

And Storm replied, "I don't know if I really trust her." She said some mean things about her that I don't remember to this day, but I wondered why Storm told me those things considering that I said considering I spoke pleasantly about my old manager.

I think Storm wanted me to work in a way where I just did things, but I wasn't able to do that in the way that she wanted. There was no training or clear expectations or guidelines to what she wanted. She managed me minimally because she had too much going on but I had a lot of questions.

I wasn't going to be someone who just followed orders and did things, I have never been that kind of person.

It was like Storm wanted me to schmooze so I'd do things in a certain way to help her control everything. This is what I started to realize.

Schmoozing is dependent on how different people want to build a relationship. Sometimes you have to start slow. Good schmoozers understand that sometimes you have to start with small talk.

Any time that I'm getting to know people, I use things that I learned from Storm. Asking "how are you?" Listening to how people state how they are, and asking more questions to deepen it.

Storm is great at small talk and Storm is great at all the stuff that kind of warms you up and gets you excited to have a conversation. There are good aspects to small talk. When you're working with people and when you're leveraging people in life and in work, people want to be able to talk about things that are not related to the task.

Schmoozing for me means, "let me spend some time getting to see how you're doing and getting to know you, and seeing what you are bringing into the space," which I think is powerful because people feel heard and listened to.

The schmoozer, when they do it right, is able to then get more work done.

Schmoozing done right is like using honey versus vinegar. Schmoozing done wrong means that I'm going to use a drop of honey, but then I have this liter of vinegar I'm going to pour on you to get things done.

Get More With Honey Than Vinegar

Honey is believing that someone else's approach to getting work done is as valuable as, and may actually be better than, your approach.

In leveraging relationships at work, it's really about understanding what's going to motivate someone else.

I find that motivating someone else is about being nice and respectful, rather than saying, "well, I'm your manager, I have authority, so you must do this."

I'm not saying there aren't circumstances where you may have to say that. I don't want to say that should never happen, but I do want to say that the critical part of using honey is that people are more likely to do something for you when they know you're respecting their work and their values.

For me, vinegar is an approach like, "I have to tell you what to do because I don't believe you want to do it."

My understanding of honey can be described with one of my favorite phrases, "unlocking the natural propensity of people to be generous." That's honey.

Vinegar is, "I don't believe you're going to be generous. I have to convince you to be generous because you're a Manipulator, too.

I think it's important to understand that people, at their core, want to be respected. They want to be valued and they want to be heard. I believe that strongly.

Using honey is being respectful to people, asking questions and being able to ascertain patterns.

I would say that a lot of my coaching is more honey than vinegar. It's all about how I ask people questions and I really listen to them.

When you're using inquiry, the tendency is for people to be like, "wait, you're really hearing me, we're working together, we're thought-partnering."

The vinegar approach is, "well, let me tell you what the solution is and let me then ask you questions to make sure you understand my solution so you're convinced of it."

That's easy to do. That's what's done in a lot of places. It's the classic approach.

People tell me I'm well-connected. I get so many damn sales emails on LinkedIn that I want to scream. "Hey, blah, blah, blah, sell, sell, sell."

I actually got one recently that I might respond to, even if I don't need any "marketing help." It's an ad about career coaching, but the person who sent it personalized it. Part of me thought, 'Oh, you took the time to actually say that you read one of my blogs and quoted it?'

Even though I don't think I need the help, I still want to respond to the humanity of it because that person used honey in their sales email to me.

Everyone else is trying to convince me, "Oh, this is a great thing. I can help you sell. I can do this."

That's a vinegar approach.

You're trying to convince me. I don't respond well to that and I don't think most people do.

Going with the honey approach is often slower. If you think about honey versus vinegar, honey is more powerful.

I was pre-med, and this is chemistry. Pour honey, it's slow. Poor vinegar, it's faster because it's a lighter liquid.

Vinegar in its properties can be shocking. Honey stays and endures once it coats you even though it's slow.

Honey is one of the most natural sweeteners we can use that is actually good. As somebody who's dealt with allergies for way longer than I'd ever care to admit, honey is a really good way for my body to treat my allergies because it's soothing. It's bringing what bees are getting from the local pollen to get my body to be acclimated to it.

Vinegar obviously has good properties too, like apple cider vinegar.

But what do we mainly use vinegar for? It's a disinfectant. It kills things. I'm not saying that's a bad thing.

I'm saying that approach has its merit, but in a lot of circumstances, like not being in "war time," I try to lead with honey.

Leading with vinegar is different. Vinegar works, it can be valuable. But using vinegar has a tendency to lead to lots of unintended consequences because a lot of other things get burnt in its path.

I'm not one of those people who say you should never use vinegar and you should always use honey. That's not true. Because if I used honey in a fight, I might have a problem.

But when it comes to getting along with people, using honey is the better approach.

Trust Is Earned

Trust is earned by the integrity of how you act and what you say.

I think the Manipulator doesn't do that. The Manipulator says what they need to say to get you to do what they want you to do. The Manipulator manipulates.

A true leader collaborates and meets people where they are. They know how to nurture, coach and nudge to get people to where they should be.

It's an act of moving people along rather than an act of bludgeoning them.

I personally like to start with trusting people more often than not. I'm not saying that I trust everyone 100%. I think I've learned to be pragmatic, as a native New Yorker and from my lived experience.

If you trust people 100%, sometimes you can get burned. I'd probably say I'm at 80 - 90% most times. You have to hold back sometimes. I believe you have to have some level of discretion.

But my orientation is to lead more with trust. I believe in the inherent goodness of people. I believe that you want to "unlock the natural propensity of people to be generous."

For me, it starts with my own orientation, because that's all I can control. I do believe other people's guardrails start to come down if I lead from a place of trust.

But sometimes you have to fight fire with fire when it comes to somebody like Storm.

Sometimes you have to stand up for yourself. When you're with Storm, you have to say, "that's just un-acceptable and here's why." You could still do it in a respectful way, and not get in a shouting match or anything like that. You have to hold your ground when you encounter the Manipulator.

This is where you can say, "hey, I've got vinegar in my bag of tricks too."

Personally, I just don't lead with vinegar.

But you want a little bit of vinegar? I got some.

I got good vinegar too. I got rice vinegar because I'm Filipino.

●●•...•●

People say things to me like, "Ron, I'm indebted to you. You built a relationship with me in such a way that I trust you deeply. Ron, your reputation precedes you. People trust you."

How do I build trust? Just how I said: I listen and I hear patterns. I provide advice when necessary. I make space. I give people my full attention, not just with my eyes, but my being. I lead from a place of trust.

That story you're telling me? I'm going to trust it. I might ask questions if something is unclear to me, but I have an orientation where I take the story that some-one tells me at face value and believe it is true.

Does that mean it's always true? Of course not. I ask questions if something doesn't sound clear to me. I've often found, in the building of trust, that people will tell you more if you ask the right questions. There's an opportunity if people hedge. You go, "hmm, well, why are you hedging? What's going on?"

It's pretty fascinating to see if folks start to talk in circles.

I think I've learned about the building of trust through interviewing thousands of people. The Manipulator, Storm, was one of the first people who I learned from on how to facilitate an interview well. I learned way back then not to use as much body language. I was told to keep a poker face when you do it.

I understand the science of that, yet at the same time, it would be weird if I'm trying to build rapport with someone. It would be weird If all I do is stare with an unmoving facial expression. I smile and use a little head nod. I think people want some kind of acknowledgement.

One of the things I think I've learned about trust is that you have to do all these little things in order to build it, and everyone's a little bit different. The thing about building trust, ultimately, is about being insatiably curious about people and believing their truth.

I don't have to agree with their truth. That's different. Someone could be living their life differently to the way that I value. But I've learned to believe what people tell me. I'm not the first person who has said that. But I believe what people tell me.

People will notice when you start to do this. What you can control and what you know and who you are comes through authentically.

My reputation in this space is great. People have told me again and again, "Ron, people trust you because you're authentic as hell. It comes across in your writing. It comes across in the way you talk, it comes across in the way you look. It comes across in the way that people talk about you."

You can't fake that shit. You can't.

One of the things I've learned about trust is learning to be secure in myself.

This is a little bit Freudian here, but I think Storm and the Manipulator archetype of Storm is deeply insecure. The schmoozing comes from a place of manipulation, and not being secure about themselves. There's no other way to say it.

As I've gotten more secure in myself, it's allowed my authenticity to flourish.

I could not have created this book at 32. I was not as authentic and secure then.

But 47-year-old Ron? Oh shit. That is a secure, authentic person.

That doesn't mean I'm perfect. It doesn't mean I don't make mistakes. It doesn't mean that I'm not learning.

But I'm grounded.

Be Decisive

The other thing about the Manipulator is being decisive.

I'm not always decisive and I haven't always been decisive. One of the things I've learned from the Manipulator is that you're never going to have perfect information about everything.

Sometimes you just have to make a decision when you're the leader. You can have imperfect information and you're going to have lots of people telling you things. I think the Manipulator doesn't care about being liked.

One of the things I've learned in counter to the Manipulator is something my wife and I talk about a lot. You get a lot more with honey than vinegar.

I realized that the Manipulator's approach is with that vinegar.

At my old workplace, people didn't want to say that Storm being controlling made it difficult to do work. And it built a culture of mistrust. It built a culture of people feeling like they had pins and needles. It built a culture of people thinking that everything had to go through this one person.

Storm's strategy was like, "I want to build this culture because I want to protect the big boss."

This protection of the big boss ended up being counter-productive. There were things that the big boss probably needed to know through the filter of Storm that weren't ever going to get to her because people didn't trust her enough to tell her things.

●●•...•●

You're in a lot of trouble when people start to question your intent. I see that in all the different ways I navigate the world. At the workplace, inside my company, with clients, and with candidates.

When folks start to doubt your intent, boy, you're in shit's creek.

I doubted Storm's intent because I didn't see any action from her around, "hey, you're not good at this skill. And I don't think you can do it."

There was no support, nor what I thought was a conflu-ence of evidence to prove that. She said, "I needed this and you didn't do it."

I reasoned, "But you didn't model it for me and teach me how to do it."

I started to doubt her intent about how she said she still wanted to keep me there because she believed I did good work. That intent was like a Band-Aid that started to get more ripped off over time when she began to have me being managed by a junior leader and reorganizing Microsoft Office folders.

That's when the hammer hit the nail and I stopped trusting Storm's intent. I thought, 'There's value for me here at this workplace, but she's not a person of her word. Now Storm's giving me work responsibility that she would have given a college intern. She gave this task to a 15-year professional."

I knew from then on that I couldn't trust Storm anymore.

I ended up doing a social media post about what hap-pened in this situation, without naming names. Actu-ally, when I look at my LinkedIn impressions, it's one of my top 50 posts. Surprise, surprise.

Storm reached out to me because she still follows me on social media even though I no longer follow her directly.

She wrote to me about an hour or two after the post and said, "hey, it's been a long time and so much has happened. I hope you're well and you have a new job and it'd be nice to catch up."

But I'm not an idiot. I thought, 'It's a little bit too close for comfort with you reaching out after all these years and the timing of my post. I ain't a dummy. You wanted reconciliation. You want to forget.'

She was schmoozing with me to try to get me to talk.

Nah, you're not talking to 32-year-old Ron any more. You're talking to secure, authentic, wise, Yoda, Charles Xavier, Magneto Ron. This Ron doesn't fucking play.

I didn't respond for a couple of days and then I just responded with honey. I said, "it's great to hear from you, Storm. Hope things are well. Congrats on your new role. Best of luck to you and look forward to staying in touch." Honey.

If Storm would have followed up and replied, "I appreciate that. I would still love to catch up. There's a lot we need to talk about." I probably would have taken that opening, but I've not heard from her since then.

I took it as her just wanting to schmooze with me to see if I was going to offer up and want to chat.
Nope.

●●•••●●

Manipulators are good when you need to get shit done. They're very action oriented. You can leverage the Manipulator if there is a result that you want and your values aren't lining up with it.

I'm not saying the Manipulator never has values that align with what you want to do. You just have to tread lightly because if all you do is focus on the Manipulator and the result, sometimes there can be other things that are burnt in the path of the Manipulator getting things done.

The worst thing is having to then salvage other relationships when the Manipulator gets something done for you.

But the big thing to learn from the Manipulator is about the decision making process and being decisive.

Then there's this whole idea of balancing wanting to be respected by others and being liked. I do believe there is a value in knowing that if you care too much about being liked, then you're not always going to make the right decision. Being liked may mean that you're not valuing the very impact you want to have in the work you're doing.

I'll give a clear example. In schools, you might want to be liked by the adults in the building, but do you want to be liked by the students? That's different. Are you doing what's necessary in schools and school districts and charters for the betterment of adults, or for the betterment of kids? Who do you ultimately want to be liked or respected by?

People in schools, in my experience, often pick adult comfort. "I want to be liked. I don't want people to be mad at me. I don't want to deal with that noise."

You know what the Manipulator says? "Fuck that shit, I care about kids, I want to do what's right for kids."

Yet, there is a balance with it. You can't just say "fuck the adults, I want to do what's right for kids" Because without the adults, you can't do what's right for kids.

It's this balance of learning how to use vinegar and honey. Both have their purpose.

● ● ● ... ● ● ●

I do have these moments when I think about my work, being 47, and the legacy that I'm building. How would people talk about me at my wake?

Being a Manipulator means that, ultimately, when you die, you're not going to have anybody at your funeral.

If that's the way you want to live, God bless you. I know it's harsh.

No one shows up to that wake. If they do, it's silently. They're nodding, they say pleasantries, they're schmoozing, they won't say anything deep.

If that's the way you want to live your life, that's cool. But that's not a way to leave a legacy.

Lead with honey, because you get more by respecting people than by belittling people.

You can't wait for the perfect time to make a decision. I think that's something I learned from the Manipulator about decisiveness.

Getting to know people's values and stories is as important as getting them to do the work.

Manipulators get shit done. And you want to balance respecting people along the way to get shit done in the best way.

● ● ● . . . ● ● ●

Thank you, Storm. You taught me many important lessons! I wish you well, and I hope you have now found a way to get more with honey than vinegar.

CHAPTER FOUR

Straight Shooter – Deb Lang

A Straight Shooter doesn't give a fuck about your feelings. But they do care about improving you. And when you get to where you really should be, the Straight Shooter will give you a pat on the back or a fist bump and say, "I knew you could do it."

The Straight Shooter is the person in your life who tells you the truth. They might curse, but they're not going to hold back when it comes to letting you know what they're seeing about you and the impact that it's having. It's almost like how castor oil can be good for you, but it doesn't always feel good going down.

I think of the Straight Shooter as someone that gives you unfiltered, unvarnished truth and advice about your life. They're not going to dress it up and make it all pretty. They're not going to try and figure out how to share their feedback with you in a way that you like. Instead, they'll say to you, "no, this is what I fucking see. Do some shit about it."

The Straight Shooter is the person who grabs you and shakes you to wake you up.

Deb Lang has always been the Straight Shooter in my life. In all of the years that I've known Deb, she's always come out with whatever needs to be said. Whether she's giving advice or sharing her opinion, she doesn't worry about how it's going to land with me or other people.

Sometimes, Deb will say something that may not go down well with a group or a person. But it's always coming from the right place. With Deb, it's like she's saying, "hey, I'm seeing something about you that I think could be better, or could make others better." She doesn't shy away from that, which is what I love about her.

I think it was 2005 when I first met Deb. It was in my first couple of months at an organization called New Leaders, a national education nonprofit. I had to travel to Chicago for work and Deb was one of the leadership coaches there that was supporting aspiring principals through a program. So, that's where I got to meet her.

I remember Deb and a couple of the other leadership coaches and I went out to dinner at some really nice Italian restaurant in the city. I sat down with Deb and I just remember thinking, 'Oh my God,' because she was saying whatever she wanted to.

She was giving relationship advice to my manager at the time, and saying all kinds of things. I just remember thinking, 'this Deb, there's just no filter here. She's just going to say it.' I was just chuckling and thinking that this was someone I wanted to keep in my life because I didn't have many people like that around me in 2005. I didn't know anyone who would just say something to you without waiting.

At the time, I would have been around 30, so I was coming into my maturation, into the beginning of more foundational years for me. Now, I think of meeting Deb as an important thing that happened in my life. Even then I knew, 'this is someone that will push me and tell me things that other people are either too nice or too afraid to say to me.'

From that point, whenever I went to Chicago I would go out of my way to ask Deb if we could have dinner or chat over lunch for 30 minutes and catch up.

She'd always start off by saying, "Ron, how are things going? How's your love life?" All the things that I think any wise aunt or maternal figure would ask, right?

Keeping in touch with Deb worked well because I worked in New Leaders for seven years and she was always around. Aside from working on the Chicago team, she also worked for the national team, so she'd come to New York and I'd find opportunities to go and meet up with her there too.

Maybe we lost track a little once I left New Leaders, but I then rediscovered our relationship through the magic of Facebook. I remember finding her and thinking, 'oh wait, Deb Lang's on Facebook?' So I added her and I just remember that feeling of 'oh shit, I haven't been in contact with you.' She was so lovely and I got her cell phone number again. I simply said, "we should do lunch." And we did.

We then re-established our relationship because she always made time for me. Even as I've been writing this book, I realized, 'wait, I haven't spoken to her in a minute, let me go reach out.'

She responded within 24 hours. I told her how I've learned so much that I want to share with her and how she's been such a mentor to me. She was kind of self-deprecating, she was like "well I don't know how wise I am, but I'm happy to eat with you Ron."

It's actually been really easy to keep in contact with Deb because I've always just said to her, "hey, I'd love to catch up," and she's always made time for me. It's really been that simple.

● ● ● ... ● ● ●

I experienced most of Deb's straight shooting while I worked at New Leaders. If I'm honest, I don't know how ready I was for Deb's advice when I was in my early 30s. But I would say Deb really helped my career after we re-established our relationship via Facebook and began to sit down over meals in 2018 and 2019.

I was working at Edgility full-time and she heard a lot about what I was doing. One day she said, "Ron, you're doing so many amazing things. Look at the network you have. But if you're not thinking about it already, you better start banking some stuff, because you have a family."

And to be honest, I just wasn't thinking like that. In her wisdom, Deb made me realize that I was in the crucial earning years of my career. She made me realize that I had better take advantage and start saving to build a nest egg.

She said, "45 to 55, make it happen, because you don't want to be 55 and not have started banking wealth."

I think she gave me a kick in the ass with that conversation and subsequent others. From how I grew up, I had just thought that I would keep working until I retired and then things would magically fall into place. I'd gotten to a place where I could start building wealth but I wasn't really being conscious of why I should be doing it.

I had said to Deb, "I'm just going to work hard, do really well and things will come to me." But she answered that with, "no Ron, you have to work even harder. You should have this mindset over the next 10 years of your life. Find opportunities to do more for your family."

I realized that Deb's advice was going to set me up for the next ten plus years of my life if I did something with it. I knew I had to do something because, with Deb, it was coming from someone who was retired, and, at least from what I saw, living a pretty good life in her older years.

I had this feeling that was like, "wait a second," because I haven't always been someone who likes to plan ahead.

Deb's straight shooting made me realize that my life wasn't just about me anymore. It was about my wife and my daughters and I had to start thinking ahead and building wealth to do right by them.

A Truth Teller

I've always felt that Deb is a truth teller. I've found that Deb has a natural impatience and she doesn't wait to say something. From what I've seen, people often wait for the right moment to give someone advice but sometimes that moment just doesn't happen the way that they want.

What I appreciate about Deb Lang is that she just makes the moment happen. She just tells you.

I'm going to be honest, some folks could find the Straight Shooter's advice disconcerting. It's often unsolicited relationship or life advice. Deb is that person in your life, as a truth teller, who is just going to tell you what she sees and, like it or not, you've got to take it or leave it.

I decided to take it because Deb has always said the kinds of things that other folks try to say but can't because of their timing or how they package things. Sometimes you need to feel a little bit unstable to be able to see things around you.

Sometimes when you're at a point of feeling stable and calm, you don't always hear other people's advice. At least in my experience. But the way that Deb gives advice is like, "hey, wake up, wake up, this is it."

In my circle of champions, Deb Lang is always going to be the person who doesn't wait for the right moment. We all need truth tellers in our lives. I don't know if I would have ever gotten Deb's advice from someone else in my life. And I appreciate that.

I think the moment that Deb's advice really clicked was in that summer of 2018 when she made me ask myself, "what am I doing in my career and my life that continues to build that wealth?"

Without Deb's truth-telling, I could argue that I would not have written this book. I would have told myself that I didn't have the time, that I was too busy. It's so easy to make an excuse, but a lot of times the Straight Shooter can tell you something that gets stuck in your head. For me it was, '45 to 55,' What am I doing to build more wealth?'

Right now, I'm 47. So I tell myself, 'Make that extra time, Ron,' because if I take Deb's advice and keep putting in this work now, I'll be alright when I'm 55. And I'll be able to make different life decisions in the future.

That's what Deb was trying to make me realize. The Straight Shooter knows that telling you the truth will only help you.

A Motivator

I'm pretty diligent when it comes to choosing the people who I spend time with. I really enjoy spending time with Deb because I get to hear about her kids. I get to hear about how she's riding off into her retirement and doing things. I get to talk a little bit too, before she says, "all right Ron, tell me where you are."

I also know I'm not the only one she does this with. She's kept in contact with so many people since retiring. At New Leaders, she had a reputation as someone who always told people what they needed to hear. Like a motivational coach.

I just feel very grateful to be someone who gets to talk with Deb. I know when I sit down with her, she's going to go into coaching mode. She listens, and then she's going to say something that just cuts through all the noise. "Here it goes, Ron." and I go, "okay, got it."

I have a lot of warm, nurturing, lovely people in my life so I've always found the conversations I've had with Deb to have a different energy. Our convos have always made me motivated to do something.

She's always just been like "come on, fucking do it." Sometimes she doesn't even have to say anything, her presence says it all. She doesn't even have to be loud with it. It's tough, but at the same time, she'll give me this feeling like, "it's no problem, I got you." Then, when you do whatever it is that she motivated you to do, she'll congratulate you and pat you on the back.

I love that shit because there are times when we are all going to have a level of self-doubt about what we are doing. My self-doubt appeared today when I was working out at the gym. I was on the seventh and final rep of my third set of heavy squats and I started making excuses. I was doubting myself, thinking 'six was really hard, seven is gonna be too tough. I did deadlifts before this, I'm tired.'

So, in moments like that, I always think back to the motivating conversations I've had with Deb. She's always been like, "No, Ron, do the fucking work. Trust me, in the long run, it'll be better for you." So, I let out this primal scream and I jumped out of that fucking squat.

Wants To Improve You

There are folks in college sports and pro sports who coach from a place of tough love. Deb gives tough love too. Unlike other people in my circle of champions, I would say that Deb Lang is not warm and fuzzy. That's not what you get when you meet her.

Deb is like 6'2" or 6'3", and she's got a big presence. Some people find it really intimidating when she speaks with them. I must admit, I felt kind of intimidated too, when I first met Deb.

In my experience, it's really unusual to see tall women working in K-12 education, so Deb's height was the first thing I noticed when I met her. She was just this really tall woman with a Chicago accent.

I'm not tall by any stretch of the imagination. I'm barely 5'8. So I think seeing her height and the way she came into the room, it gave me the sense that there was just a presence about her. I don't know how else to describe it, she just has a big presence. And that can be intimidating sometimes.

So when I think about our first meeting and how she appeared, I knew she was going to be demanding. But I didn't know she was going to be warm.

Now I know that deep down, Deb really cares about helping people do well. She cares about helping them to improve. From talking with people, I know that Deb helped a bunch of people that she worked with at New Leaders.

There's at least 100 plus people that she's impacted and she probably still keeps in contact with them all today.

When I first started at New Leaders, it was early in my career and I was thinking, 'what does hiring for this school leaders program even look like?'

I remember talking a lot with Deb and other people on her team about how it was all new for me and how much I was learning.

There was a moment when she told me, "Ron, I gotta tell you something. Trust yourself."

She told me that I shouldn't be intimidated by the people like her who had done the job for a long time. But 30 year old Ron was a little afraid of all these folks who were almost twice my age.

But Deb turned all that on its head by telling me, "no, you have something to offer here. Don't let what you perceive of us get in the way of that. You have a truth to tell too. So trust yourself." That's always stuck with me.

● ● ● ● ● ● ●

There are many variations of hot chocolate. Stay with me here for a second.

Some hot chocolates are really sweet and light, but Deb is like a strong chocolate, which is not necessarily for everybody.

Some people like the "Dunkin' Donuts hot chocolate," type of person. It's just light and sweet and that's how they like to get feedback from the people they have around them. Personally, I like a really strong, cacao hot chocolate where you melt dark chocolate and then you sugar it up.

Deb Lang is strong, but still warm. Not everybody likes her kind of intensity, but it's like this warm intensity. She's strong but she's still going to make sure you're nurtured.

When it comes to Deb, I often think of a term that gets thrown around a lot in education circles. Deb is a 'warm-demander.' She demands, she's stern, but she's warm about it.

Sometimes you need someone in your circle of champions to give you tough love. Sometimes I think you just need a different way of having things shared with you to help you improve. And that's what a Straight Shooter does.

Is Wise

When I was starting at Edgility I think there were moments when I wasn't quite sure about my footing. I was
coming in and learning how to sell and doing all these
things that were still new to me. A lot of people were
telling me "no."

One of the things I remember Deb telling me at the time
was, "Ron, you're so good with people. Why does getting
a no throw you off when you're trying to get business?
Why is that a big deal for you?"

After hearing that from Deb I had this "aha moment." I
realized that she was right.

I realized that my fear of the 'no' and the trepidation that
I had when it came to selling was coming from a place
where I was thinking, 'God, it sucks to hear no.' So, I just
had to reorient myself.

Deb would say, "Ron, you gotta take no as 'not
yet'." She'd say, "I've seen you work, and when people
really get to know you, they can't say no to you". I remember thinking, 'oh, that's true.' She just shot
straight through it all. She just went for it. Deb, with
the tough love, goes straight to the thing that needs to
be said and her wise advice is always impactful.

When Deb and I talk, there's not usually much back and forth between us, right? She's just like, "here it goes. I'm gonna lay it all at your feet because I know you."

I've gotten a lot of amazing wisdom nuggets just from speaking with Deb over the years. Once I let my guard down and she asked questions, there would always be things that would just come up.

I go back to when we were starting to have lunch right before the pandemic. Once again, I was at a point in Edgility where I was trying to figure stuff out.

I was doing business development and I was selling, but there were some leadership challenges there that I was wrestling with internally.

I felt like I was doing everything on my own without much help. So Deb looked me in the eye and she said, "Ron, something I know about you is that you're so used to doing work on your own because you're really self-sufficient, and I admire that about you, but if there's something you need, why aren't you telling your manager?"

I recall saying something like, "ahh, she's busy and I don't know." But Deb came back and said , "Ron, you don't know until you ask. How's your relationship with her?"

I said, "it's good, but I don't want to..." But Deb replied, "Ron, let me cut through the noise for you. At this point in your life, if you don't ask for what you need and something doesn't happen, it's your responsibility."

So I did it. And my manager was open to it and I got the help I needed. That was really pragmatic advice that I got from Deb. You can't wait. And that's stuck with me as I've gotten older.

Sometimes I think what my Straight Shooter has done for me with her wisdom is help me get out of my own way.

Makes Time For You

I often think back to the time I met Deb in 2005 and how we still have a relationship today in 2023. A big part of that is because Deb has always made time for us to get together.

Soon after I re-established my relationship with Deb, she moved to New York to be closer to her family. I remember we were talking about having a meal and she said "Ron, surprise me. What kind of food do you want to get?" I was like, "have you tried Filipino food?"

She had never tried it so we went to a spot in New York that was near her. When I think about her making time for me, a lot of the time we've spent together has been over a good meal, whether it's lunch or dinner.

I saw a lot of Deb's caring side when she agreed to let me take her to the Filipino restaurant. It was one of those beautiful moments. I wish I could have recorded it. She just said, "Ron, I trust you. Whatever this is, I'll try it."

The meal that we were having was called 'sisig.' It's put together with the parts of a pig that are not considered 'desirable.' Those parts are chopped up, grilled, and spices and other things are added to the dish to make it taste delicious.

When we got to the restaurant, I said, "Deb, you're going to love sisig." She replied, "All right, I trust you." Then I explained to her that the dish is all the parts of the pig that aren't usually eaten, like its snout, its feet and its entrails.

But when she tasted it, I asked her what she thought. She replied, "Ron, this is absolutely delicious."

Later she said that she would never have thought that the meal would have been delicious because of how I described it to her. But Deb has this willingness to try. A willingness to try things and trust.

That moment at the Filipino spot really deepened my relationship with Deb. It was like she said, "Ron, I'll try this food, and hey, if I don't like it I'll tell you. But I'm willing to try it because you and I have built a trusting relationship and I want to get to know you more."

From that meeting, I knew that if I trusted Deb with her advice, she trusted me with my advice too. It was a two way street.

And that moment would never have happened if Deb hadn't made time for us to meet.

● ● ● ● ● ● ●

I think the progress of my career would have been slower if I hadn't met Deb. As my Straight Shooter, she's someone who's been like an accelerator in my life. A real Straight Shooter is like an enzyme that you need to move to your action potential, right?

I keep going back to the advice Deb gave me about building wealth. Now, I realize that I wouldn't be a homeowner without the kind of money that I make. My Straight Shooter kicked me to do that.

Without Deb's advice, I wouldn't have written this book. I wouldn't be a senior leader that is scaling a company to hopefully 50 million in the next 10 years.

So I take the advice I get from Deb really seriously. When you get advice from the Straight Shooter, it then opens you up to be more attentive to the opportunities that are often right before you.

Without my Straight Shooter, I think I would have been less likely to see, or not willing to see, the opportunities that were before me.

My Straight Shooter gave me a big energy push. It was almost like I was running the hundred yard dash and Deb Lang was there to help me break the world record. She gave me a big push for the first 20 yards, and then I took care of the rest.

● ● ● ● ● ● ●

To find your Straight Shooter, you have to find the person at work, or in your life, who is willing to tell the truth all the time. You have to find somebody who does that because they deeply care about people.

A Straight Shooter, at times, is like a really good personal trainer or a therapist. They could be someone who's a senior leader at an organization, who's seen it all, and just loves mentoring people.

I often think you can identify a Straight Shooter just by noticing how someone walks into a room. They are the people who have such a presence that they are intimidating at first. But when you sit down with them, there is a caring about them that belies the big intimidating presence they have when they come into a room.

● ● • • • • ● ●

You don't get that jet fuel acceleration boost without a Straight Shooter. I think there are moments in our life when we need to grow and start moving. Some of this is like a physics concept. The Straight Shooter allows you to see your inertia and gets you off your ass.

There can be a lot of moments in life when you are moving really incrementally, and sometimes you need a nudge to leverage your skills, and the people around you, to flourish and do whatever you need to do.

The Straight Shooter is the person that gives you a swift kick in the back to get you off the sofa.

Without a Straight Shooter you won't have someone who's not going to wait around to tell you what you need to hear. I think one of the things you can't do in life is wait for the right time and the Straight Shooter doesn't do that. They just shoot straight, like, "here it goes. A to B. Here's the thing I'm going to tell you."

I have found that most people will just wait for the right moment. That's not always a bad thing. But when I think about the different things you need in order to accelerate in your life and career, you need someone that can give you a swift kick in the butt at times.

●●•••••●●

The benefit of having a Straight Shooter in your life is that they will give you the advice that you need when you need it.

Often I found that Deb gave me advice that I didn't expect to get. But it was exactly the right place and the right time to get it.

I don't think there was ever a moment when I went to Deb because I actually needed her advice. But whenever I met her, there was always something she straight shot at me that I needed at that moment.

I'm having lunch with her in a couple of weeks just to catch up. I know she's going to have advice for me. I have zero idea what the hell she's going to tell me. That's the point, right?

She's not the person in my circle of champions who I'll go to when I'm like "wait, there are these three things I want to weigh up." We just sort of banter and she's always going to see through stuff and say, "Ron, here's what I see."

I don't necessarily say, "hey, here's something I'm struggling with, let me go to Deb for it." So what I appreciate about Deb Lang and the Straight Shooter archetype is that they'll give you what you didn't know you needed.

No one is expected to have all the right answers when they're navigating their career. Sometimes you need to just sit with someone who's going to listen to you and give you their unfiltered advice.

Now, is that for everybody? It depends on where you are in terms of maturity. I think I have reached a point in my life where I like tough love.

Not every person in your circle of champions has to be someone who nurtures you like, "ok, let's move at your pace." The Straight Shooter gets you out of your comfort zone. And you need someone in your life who does that.

● ● ● ● ● ● ●

Deb, thank you for fucking believing in me, and helping me get out of my comfort zone, to improve in my career and my life.

CHAPTER FIVE

No-Nonsense Nurturer – Kevin Bryant

There's a space for a No-Nonsense Nurturer in every-one's life. Or there should be, anyway. Mine is Kevin Bryant.

Kevin's recent departure from the company where I work has left a significant void, and that's what prompted me to reflect on his leadership style and the impact he had on our team's collective success.

Kevin and I worked closely together, always engaging in regular conversations about our search work and bouncing ideas off of each other. He can be quite guarded about personal matters but he was always direct with his communication relating to work, thus providing a no-nonsense approach to getting things done.

Kevin's directness and emphasis on honesty and trust in relationships made his input invaluable. His relent-less pursuit of results combined with the ability to build strong relationships with his team created a culture of accountability and trust that ultimately drove the organization to new heights.

As Kevin moves to a new role as a managing partner at another search firm, I believe his no-nonsense nurturing approach will continue to be an effective strategy for driving progress and success.

●●•••••●●

Before I first encountered Kevin Bryant, he was already renowned as Director of Recruitment at a big charter school network in the Northeast and his reputation preceded him. It was not until we both received job offers at my current search company that we had a chance to speak.

He reached out to me and said he would like to pick my brain on something and learn about my perspective, having heard good things about me and my prior consulting work for Edgility.

From my first interaction with Kevin, I realized he valued directness and clarity in communication. While his approach somewhat differed from Deb Lang, he was equally focused on building relationships based on trust and honesty and didn't like to beat around the bush.

At the time, I had already accepted the offer to work at Edgility so I was kind of urging him to join in a way that didn't try to sell it. I told the truth and answered his questions as honestly and forthrightly as possible. Kevin asked me questions like, "Ron, what's your experience here? I'm a Black man, does Edgility care about diversity, equity, and inclusion the way that I do, the way that you do?"

I told him the truth, that the company was still in progress. I said that I couldn't say they cared about things in the way that both of us did, but I thought that he would value the workplace and what he could get out of it.

That first interaction between us didn't start with any small talk. We got right into it. We were 30 minutes in, and he was shooting direct questions that I answered as truthfully as I could. That moment painted a picture and set the tone for how our future conversations would go.

● ● ● ... ● ●

In office meetings, Kevin would share his thoughts and opinion with clarity and precision. I deeply respect his economy of words. He doesn't waste time on meaningless words and will convey his thoughts and opinions without sugarcoating. He tells you things as they are, and to me, that is how he shows he cares about you. He will respect your time and tell you the things you need to hear.

That is the true mark of a No-Nonsense Nurturer. It's like, "I don't have a lot of words to spend with you, so I am going to tell it like it is. But that's how I show I care about you, because I don't waste my time and I certainly don't want to waste yours."

That's Kevin in a nutshell.

He builds relationships by being transparent about his thoughts and opinions which can be unnerving to some people. When I think about how people communicate, Kevin is on the other end of the spectrum. He may not ask many questions, instead, he will just say, "This is what I think, and what do you think about that?"

He doesn't always wait to ask all the questions and gather all the information before he shares his own thoughts, which can be both a strength and a weakness. What we both share in common is how we can be very strategic and often don't explain every tiny detail of how we are doing things to other people. That's because we both move fast, he is as whip-smart as I am.

There is a drawback to Kevin's approach, however. It can lead to taking certain things for granted and assuming that others are at the same level of understanding as he is. I once approached Kevin about this and coached him to slow down a bit to ensure that other teams and departments have the time to chew up his information and keep up with him. While his quick thinking can be a great asset, it's important to strike a balance that allows everyone to fully participate in the process and contribute to the team's success.

When I see positive things, I say them to someone to keep the relationship on good terms. Kevin is not afraid to shake things up a bit and be disruptive. He's like, "No, I'm going to tell you what I think, I'm going to share this feedback. If it affects our relationship we'll figure it out, but I'm going to be really direct with you." Kevin's way of showing he cares is very distinct from many others who I've met in my career.

It can be tough to find someone who exhibits this kind of directness with love and care. Sometimes, we have moments when we just need someone who is going to show love and care in a kind and gentle manner but other times only the direct approach will work.

●●•••●●

One of the most important moments when I learned from Kevin was when I faced a situation with a client where I should have been more direct before taking action. Instead of being honest and saying, "I feel uncomfortable about what you just said and what you're doing," I decided to bypass the client altogether because I didn't trust them to do the right thing.

During a joint search at work, there was a candidate that the client was hesitant to move forward with due to an informal reference they received from an organization that the candidate would be working closely with.

The situation involved a Black female candidate. Kevin and I discussed it and he suggested that I hold off on contacting her. I found the whole situation unacceptable. To be honest, I get triggered by these kinds of things that get into processes and often affect BIPOC folks.

I spoke to Kevin and my initial inclination was how bullshit it all was and how I felt obliged to tell this to the candidate. But it blew up in my face.

In hindsight, it was a bad strategic move because the candidate ended up talking to the source of information directly because she had a relationship with this person.

That person was caught off guard and, as it turns out this person is a funder in the community of the organization. Consequently, our client was unhappy.

I had good intentions to protect the candidate and Kevin understood it from my perspective but also suggested that we should not have acted so rashly. This was a moment of nurturing. He was able to listen and understand from my perspective and we both realized the impact of our actions on the client relationship and apologized. Kevin took part of the bullet for me which helped us maintain the client relationship. In the end, we were able to place a different but equally qualified candidate after they decided they just were not going to move that first candidate forward.

This is where Kevin's wisdom as a No-Nonsense Nurturer made a profound impact on me. He advised that I should at least have given the client the opportunity to hear my perspective and discuss my plans, so it could have been a conversation rather than looking like I was going behind their back.

My intention to protect people of color was in the right place but my strategy wasn't effective. I am unapologetic about why I did what I did, because protecting people of color, particularly Black women, is a non-negotiable for me. I wouldn't change what I did but I might have changed how quickly I did it if I'm gonna be honest with you.

But this was what Kevin was saying to me at that moment. Based on his experience as a Black man himself, he understood why I did what I did. But Kevin advocated for giving it straight to the client. He wanted to tell the client that it wasn't working out and then maybe we could have hashed it out. That way, there would at least have been a chance to achieve a middle ground together.

Kevin really nurtured me at that moment. He could have easily said something like, "You fucked up, Ron." Instead, he said, "I understand why you did it." That was the first-moment big moment when I knew that we were going to have each other's backs.

● ● ● ... ● ●

In a circle of champions, it's important to have someone who can understand your feelings and be direct with you, while also caring about achieving results. Kevin, as a No-Nonsense Nurturer, has a blend of both.

Kevin embodies the archetype of someone who cares deeply about results and getting things done. Anytime

I worked with him, I have had zero doubts that he will see it through and I don't say that about a lot of people. Through the searching we have done together, I am a first-hand witness to how he has always interacted with his clients in a direct, no-nonsense manner that cuts to the chase.

This no-nonsense approach is crucial for one's career because sometimes you need someone to tell you exactly what needs to be done and why, without any fluff. At the same time, a No-Nonsense Nurturer also cares about what is going on in your personal life knowing that it impacts your professional life. They are a balance between being directive and strategic while also showing care and concern. Not everyone in my circle of champions has become a friend, but with Kevin, I feel comfortable letting my guard down. Kevin has indeed become a good friend.

In addition to his no-nonsense approach, Kevin is a skilled strategist. Although he can be a bit impatient, it is for good reason. If he sees something is amiss, he will call it out and will not hold back. He observes things closely and his straightforwardness comes from being able to also listen and then telling you he's had enough of it before he brings up what he thinks. He has an economy of words that comes with that directness unlike my tendency to talk for long periods and veer off-topic.

I recall a work moment when Kevin felt strongly about the efficiency of using video interviews to replace the 30-minute phone interviews we had very early on in our process at Edgility. It was a huge time suck. The search lead, partner and co-founder of the firm had reservations about it. They asked how we would build relationships with people through video interviews, which was a fair question.

Kevin acknowledged the importance of building relationships with people but suggested a process where candidates could record a video of themselves answering questions crafted by Edgility, and then the team would provide additional context and insights during their conversation with the candidates. Rather than simply providing candidates with a list of questions, the approach Kevin suggested was to show them that we were interested in getting to know them better.

The idea was to share a few questions related to the role and the organization that only we had the answers to, and then help the candidate better understand the role in the hope of getting them more excited about the opportunity.

Kevin was really direct with our co-founder about this but he also realized he needed more evidence to convince her. He drew upon the extensive research he had conducted in his previous company, he presented the pros and cons, and the process took about six months to bring in.

Kevin is strategic and assertive about what information people need to make a decision. That's why he was able to convince her even though she was really resistant to his idea at first. If he wasn't no-nonsense about it and didn't listen to her perspective and understand what she needed, i.e., nurture her, we wouldn't be using that process, which has saved us a lot of staff time, today.

●●●…●●

Kevin's directness was a bit of a cultural rarity at Edgility but I embraced it. It was nice to have someone that just cut directly to the point and was able to start a conversation, even knowing that some people might be resistant to it at first, myself included sometimes. But I always try to hear him out, having developed a deep respect for the way he thinks.

Unfortunately, Kevin's directness threw some people off at our firm. This is understandable because individuals tend to be more indirect before speaking and are not accustomed to being asked many questions.

Honestly, I think Kevin's approach did not always serve him well within our organization, even though he did a lot of beneficial things for our team. When people are not used to hearing something in a way that is not packaged for their feelings, working with someone who is direct can make them defensive.

But Kevin taught me that sometimes being direct with people is what drives progress. When you're advocating for people, you're advocating for what you believe is right and you just have to say it.

I appreciated Kevin's fearlessness. His presence taught me to be more fearless in my interactions and in expressing my views with clients.

I am now a better equity leader because of the things I learned from Kevin.

Really Cares

One time during a conversation, Kevin opened up about his nephew, whom he treats like a brother. He asked me if a client that does college access work had a list of recommended colleges for his nephew. I told him I would work on it only to realize I couldn't get it because it was proprietary information of that client. But the client gave me some information that was helpful enough. When Kevin saw that I did that for him, he started to unwind a story about his nephew and became more confident that I would show up for him.

Kevin was not only a direct person at work, but he was also a No-Nonsense Nurturer for his family. He was living in Austin at the time, but he would fly out to North Carolina to see his nephew and spend quality time with him. Not only that, but he would also offer support to him on how to get to college. Then he would be very direct about the things his nephew needed to do and the things he would follow up on with him. I saw through that nurturing side of Kevin, that he was someone who is also sensitive and caring.

That side of Kevin is rarely seen at work. He is just really direct and always wants to make progress with the tasks in front of him. I am not saying that he doesn't build relationships with people but I think it is harder for people to build relationships with him because of his direct demeanor. As a result, people have this misconception that he doesn't have a caring side. But I know it's there and this is what I want people to realize. With a No-Nonsense Nurturer, nurturing doesn't happen automatically. It's a two-way street and you have to nurture that person too.

It is a common misconception that the way to deal with a No-Nonsense Nurturer is by being no-nonsense yourself, but that's not the case at all. To see their nurturing side, you have to be willing to nurture them back. They want to be nurtured too, even if it's not their initial default. What I did for Kevin resulted in us having this special relationship of trust and that's how I became one of the first people to find out about his girlfriend, who is now his fiancé.

I even built a good relationship with her when we planned and exchanged ideas about what to get for Kevin's going away gift. My team was clueless about what to do because he was a closed book to them. But I was like, "I'm going to go ask Kiki." So I sent her a DM and told her that we wanted to surprise Kevin. Unlike the others, I also knew that he played tennis so I asked his girlfriend if he would love tennis lessons. This might sound like a simple thing to do but it says a lot about how you show up as a nurturer.

Kevin was able to show his nurturing side to me because I also nurtured him. I learned a lot about the things he loves doing, that people might not think a no-nonsense person would do. But his nurturing side is all about deeply loving, learning and being with his family and the people he loves.

Influencer

Kevin and I spoke a lot about his own conversations with our mutual manager. I helped him develop a more nurturing approach by suggesting that he use more inquiry while he taught me to balance inquiry with directness.

Kevin's directness was helpful in situations where a more gentle approach wasn't effective. However, this approach would sometimes get our manager defensive. That's where I would sometimes step in and help Kevin to be nurturing. Sometimes people need to be led gradually to understand something before they can see its full impact. From my point of view, it would have been better if my manager had been able to sit with and think about Kevin's ideas rather than dismiss them outright or get defensive.

From Kevin, what I learned to do and started doing in conversations at work was figure out how I could be direct on what I wanted to say and then use a nurturing approach like, "How does this sit with you and how can I support you on this? Because here is what I'm observing and here is how I see the impact of it."

Through this shared experience, I learned the importance of being direct and straightforward instead of going around in circles, which was my natural tendency. I realized that being direct can be a powerful tool for those who know how to respond to it. As for Kevin, I think he learned the value of leaving space for questioning after sharing feedback. It is not just about pointing out the issue but also about guiding the other toward finding a solution.

When we disagreed during leadership meetings, we would play off each other to come up with the best solution. While I might have thought my approach was good, I would try to hear out what he was saying and it would make a lot of sense. I would see how we both wanted the same result and how he was just approaching something from a different angle.

Now that Kevin is no longer with the company, I am trying to fill the gap he left in our team. None of us really fit the archetype of a No-Nonsense Nurturer and people have noticed that it is missing in leadership meetings. Working with Kevin has taught me the value of being a no-nonsense leader, even if it is not my natural tendency. It is a gift from Kevin that I now want to cultivate and provide for my team. I have seen how it can positively impact people and realized that being direct and straightforward can be a powerful tool for people that know how to respond to it.

● ● ● ● ● ● ●

I have now come to understand that being direct requires an appreciation of context, as it can make a significant difference. Let me give you an example: Sometimes when people are talking in circles, being direct can help break the impasse. It can cut through the noise and help unravel what needs to be addressed at the moment. Kevin is quite good at this and won't wait for the moment when people will be in a state of explaining things like spinning wheels. He will cut to the chase and sometimes, in some group settings, people don't like that.

Now, I have learned to embrace that, even though Kevin and I may be different in our approach, being results-oriented is where we overlap.

In terms of how directness can benefit and play out in someone's career, it is about having people in your life who can provide honest and straightforward feedback.

You need a person who can tell you what they see, even if it may be uncomfortable for you to hear. You need someone that will also nurture you at the same time when they see you need it.

It's essential to have people who are confident enough about their relationship with you that they don't have to worry about your feelings every time they are direct, because you both know that the intent is coming from a good place since you have nurtured each other many times before and built a relationship.

Other people working with Kevin wouldn't spend time getting to know him and would rather make assumptions about him. They would say he cares only about himself but that is far from the truth. If you're early in your career and you don't have the muscle to figure out things on your own yet, you need a No-Nonsense Nurturer. Find the Kevin Bryants of the world because they will be really valuable in your life. You need someone to just say, "Here's the thing you need to do. Go make it happen."

Strategic Thinker

Kevin and I were in Austin one time to hear about our company's ten-year vision. When we first got the news from our partners, I remember Kevin and I had a strong reaction to it and didn't understand why we were doing it. We were presented with numbers and figures, but we didn't have enough information to fully support the vision.

Kevin and I were balancing each other out and figuring out a strategy on how we could talk to our partners and give them feedback. It's not that we didn't believe in the vision. But, we didn't think that we had enough grounding for us to buy into it and get excited about it. And if we weren't excited about it, we couldn't make our teams excited about it either.

That was when our strategic thinking and leadership abilities came into play. We opted for a divide-and-conquer approach and tried to figure out the best way to approach each partner. With Kevin being so good at being direct, we agreed that he would talk to one of our co-founders, and I would talk to our mutual manager since I had a really good relationship with her and could say things to her in a way that she would hear.

We had this strategy of figuring out what his approach was going to be and what we were going to say based on how people responded. For me, it was about telling a story, whereas Kevin focused on understanding the numbers behind the vision. He was like, "These numbers seem to be thrown out in the left field. We need to understand why you came up with these numbers. Why 50 million, how are we coming up with stuff?"

We were doing it because we deeply cared about dismantling the systems of oppression around hiring and talent and getting more people in who looked like the community. After all, social impact organizations are always observing and at that level, if you want to scale, the numbers must add up. We were going to change the wage gaps that were happening for Black and Latina women. We wanted people to be able to build generational wealth in ways that aren't happening as much right now. This was the reason behind the 10-year vision.

But Kevin and I were both like, "We're not bought in, and we have a lot of questions." Our partners needed to go deeper into the vision, clarify their intent on why they were moving in a direction that was just not clear, and present their ideas in a way that was easy to understand.

I would have found it to be a good strategy if they thought about presenting it to us in a way that would have gotten us thinking about, 'what you know and what you don't know' Whenever you are communicating with people, you need to have the discipline to think from the perspective of the people you are presenting it to.

Now, as a company, we have started to develop a discipline that owes a lot to Kevin. Kevin's foremost concern was the "why" behind our actions as a company.

He would ask what's in it for the people and would ask that constantly and directly because if it was not properly addressed, people would perceive that they needed to get along with the program because they needed to get their paychecks. But no one that I know and respect, especially Kevin, believes that that's a way to galvanize and inspire people. At the heart of it, people will want to know the reason behind their actions.

Kevin and I may have had different approaches to the 10-year vision initially, but we found a way to strategize and figure out the best way to provide feedback for our partners.

From Kevin, I learned how essential the "why" is behind an action if you want to inspire other people.

Gets It Done

Kevin does listen, he listens to understand, and perhaps because of the breadth of his experience, he is quick to recognize the root cause of any issues at play and what needs to be done to solve them. He is truly whip-quick around this. He might have some follow-up questions but he always comes through really quickly in finding solutions.

It's not just his life experience and being in his mid-thirties that allows him to come up with quick, strategic solutions. His brain is almost wired that way. He can get really creative and kind of comes up with things. It is almost like someone who can turn clay into this incredible sculpture.

When I think about Kevin's ability to come up with creative solutions, I believe there is a part of his process that allows him to do this. I don't know what it is exactly but I can tell you an approximation of it, after the fact. There is an alchemy to Kevin's ability, like it is this incredible unconscious gift that he possesses which is something that I have always admired.

One example of that which comes to mind is how we leveraged our executive coach through the questions we asked her about the problems we were having with the way our firm was operating. We would say things like, "I'm going to ask Elsa for advice on this. Ron, you asked Elsa for her advice on that. Then we'll both talk about the advice we received and figure out how to package it for our separate conversations with our manager."

There were a lot of strategies involved in deciding what advice to seek and how to communicate the issues and the solutions. Kevin played a huge part in orchestrating the sequence of our strategy, including what to ask and how to figure out who says what when the time comes that a no-nonsense approach is appropriate.

●●•••●●

Sometimes people like Kevin, who are really silent about their work, earn a reputation of getting things done. They are reliable and effective but don't draw attention to themselves, even as they deliver results. They don't really like talking about themselves, while I'm kind of the opposite. People like Kevin, are sometimes so buried deep in what they are doing that they don't feel the need to advertise their achievements. To find a person like Kevin, you can't rely on LinkedIn or Google search. You need to rely on your network and ask for recommendations.

A No-Nonsense Nurturer is someone who is always direct with you, which means you know exactly where you stand with them. This is where the nurturing part stems from. As you build a relationship with a No-Nonsense Nurturer, they care about who you are, what your values are and what you do. It's almost like the nurturing side doesn't come to light until they feel like they can trust you to handle what they have to say.

Kevin is relentless in some ways, but also silent and thoughtful. Kevin gets things done. He won't always tell you how he gets things done, but when you ask him, he will tell you. His work pace is always like, "we have business we need to take care of and get done and we just have to keep going forward."

Another amazing thing about him is if you ask him to be a thought partner on something, or ask him about how you can approach something, he's got all the details and the relevant questions ready.

For the past four years, Kevin and I have had at least one 30-minute conversation every week. Our discussions are not always work-related. The brilliance of a No-Nonsense Nurturer is they will not waste your time with small talk. They are not about the usual kind of banter you hear from people. They will talk about things you care about, like your family.

This is one of Kevin's many gifts. He is very strategic and he has the ability to piece issues together and then come up with a number of different solutions. He understands why each of those solutions will or will not work. He will communicate all of that with you by confidently sharing his opinions and suggestions directly.

One of the things I admire most and learned about from Kevin is his resilience to move forward even when things are difficult. We can both be relentless in our pursuits but I must admit that I haven't always been strong. I get annoyed with people sometimes and check out. But Kevin sets a high bar for the right approach. He values commitment to the work and encourages me to just get the job done. He taught me that I don't need to like the people that I am working with per se. The commitment is to our own integrity. We commit to doing our work for excellence's sake, not necessarily for those people.

●●•••●●

The concept of a No-Nonsense Nurturer, as exemplified by Kevin Bryant, has proved to be a valuable asset for me in both personal and professional settings. Through my experiences at work with the No-Nonsense Nurturer, I learned the importance of direct communication, advocating for oneself, and a few more skills that can be honed with more guidance from Kevin.

Sometimes it can be daunting to navigate power dynamics or negotiate for what you want. But having someone who recognizes your strengths and exemplifies that process for you can be the key to success.

A No-Nonsense Nurturer encourages a balance between analysis and action and advocates for taking the best course of action by giving straightforward advice without overthinking. If we can incorporate this approach into any of our interactions, we can become more effective and efficient in achieving what we have set out to do.

The No-Nonsense Nurturer embodies the qualities of directness, respect and results-driven focus that can help in personal and professional challenges. For those of us who continue to work on our aspirations, our role is to seek out and cultivate relationships with someone who embodies this approach and we should strive to emulate their strengths in our own lives.

● ● ● ... ● ●

Thank you, Kevin, for helping me be a stronger equity warrior, having me advocate better for candidates and push clients' thinking on how to be more equitable. You have been valuable in my career journey as I learned how to advocate better for myself and the things I knew that I wanted, but was afraid to ask for.

CHAPTER SIX

Visionary
– Ifeyinwa "Ify" Walker

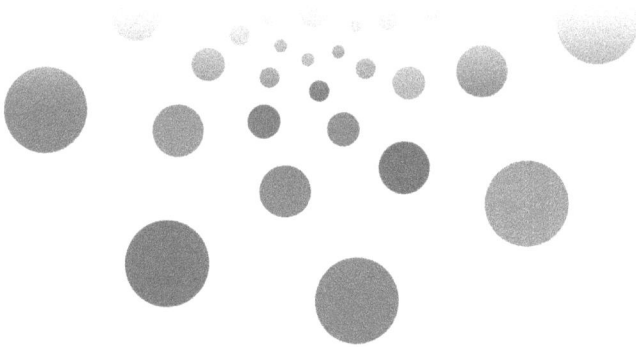

I always land on my feet.

Does that mean I'm not afraid of failing? No.

Does that mean that I don't have anxiety? No.

Do I have a fearlessness about stating what I want? Yeah.

Because why not? What's the other option? To be small? I just don't think that's the way to live your life and to think about your career.

Ifeyinwa "Ify" Walker and I first chatted via phone after I had left my job at New Leaders and she started working for my old managers. She started her own search business and she was doing a contract for my former manager's manager, Mark Murphy, in Delaware.

She reached out to me and said, "Hey, would you be interested in moving to Delaware?" What I remember about getting from Ify then was just this sense of, "I want to get to know you, are you interested?"

And it's funny, when I talked to my wife about it, she replied with, "we're not moving to Delaware. Are you out of your mind? What's in Delaware for me?"

My answer was just "okay." And so it ended up being a quick convo with Ify. But I just remember the email she sent and her voice. There was a warmth and a generosity about her.

I think when I started to see more of Ify the Visionary was when we finally met for the first time in person. I was working in Newark, so it was in early 2014, or even late 2013. I was asked by an organization that I worked at called Teach for America, of which Ify is an alum, to speak about career advice to its alumni. I was there representing the school district in my role, and I remember saying, "oh my God, Ify, it's so nice to meet you in person. You're so wonderful." There was this mutual admiration like, "Ron, I'm meeting you. Do you know your reputation?"

My response was, "what the fuck are you talking about? You're Ify, you're running your own business. Why are you gassing me up?" I'm still fascinated by it because I just have so much respect for her space.

So we took the train together and I was at a moment in my career where I was thinking, 'um, I don't know if

I'm going to be staying at Newark public schools much longer.' If you remember the Manipulator, this is where these two stories converge.

By the time I met Ify, I already knew that the writing was on the wall and I needed to leave that job. And Ify came out with , "Ron, why don't you work with me?" All I could say was, "what?"

I saw her as a visionary because she was running her own firm, and there were not a lot of Black women that I personally knew who were running their own search firms. There still aren't a lot. There are more, but at the time, in 2013, she was one of a handful that I knew. And I was just really impressed with the way she shared advice, her vision for people's careers, her vision for doing her search work and building a business.

I was particularly inspired by something she told me really early on. She said, "Ron, I care about the results of your work. How many hours do you spend? I'm not going to pay you for that." And believe it or not, that's only 10 years ago and I'd never really heard that before.

I'd been socialized to think you get paid for the amount of hours you work. She said, "no, Ron, at this point in your career, generally, you should get paid for your product. And all the work and hours it takes you to get that, it doesn't matter. So if it takes you three hours to do something, people should pay you for the value of that rather than the value of the hours." That was something that really stuck with me.

I think the thing that she said about her search firm to me disrupted this notion that people who looked like me, who looked like Ify, didn't have the talent to be in the C-suite.

She said this phrase to me that really stuck. I don't want to attribute it to Ify, but it's something she's used a lot and I've heard a lot of other people say it since then. "Genius is equally distributed, opportunity is not."

She created her search firm on that premise, "getting people in the door." To assume that folks who look like us did have the genius to do these jobs, and all we needed was an opportunity to be able to do the job, is so different from every other search firm I'd ever seen.

If you look her up, she's been in major publications. She started on LinkedIn, a "#DearBlackWomen" series. She writes, and that's how she spends a lot of her time these days, in thought leadership. The visionary part of her firm has evolved. She's not as involved in the day to day, she has other people do it but she's the thought leader, she's the external voice.

She's the one who pushes people on how you can hire in a more equitable, precise way to get our genius in the door. Usually the presumption in search is that you have to prove your genius but that is not how she models it. She's trained people on this. She's led searches. It's a 'who's who' of organizations, right?

And so I think her brilliance is the model that she has, which is even different from the model that many of us tend to have in search, because she's not cheap. She's the ultimate luxury brand that I watch. She focuses just on C-suite leaders in the social impact space. She doesn't do principal searches anymore, like when I first started with her. They are now very focused searches, and the way that she does them and the price point and the precision and the way that people are pushed in the process is amazing.

In some ways, Ify's also a No-Nonsense Nurturer. I can talk about Ify as a No-Nonsense Nurturer all day. But I think where Kevin Bryant and her are a little bit different, is that while Kevin's a visionary too, Ify's vision is off the charts. She has an ability to see 10, 15 years ahead about where the space can be. In my mind, everyone in search really follows her lead on how you think about how to do a search process for executives.

Most folks tend to do things with a "rolling process." Ify decides, "no, we got six weeks, we're going to market the hell out of this. We're going to get videos of these things and we're going to invite people." It's not stuff that's terribly common. Search tends to be very closed off to the point of, "Shh. I'm going to find out about the role. I'm going to pick you. I'm going to tap you on the shoulder."

Quite frankly, this creates a lot of inequities.

One thing I've learned from Ify, that I've started using on some level, is that visibility is a pathway to equity. People need to see that it exists. They need to be told, "hey, you can do this role," in order for them, especially those who look like me and other people of color to feel like they have a reasonable shot to apply for these roles.

We've been told, "look, if you don't have the Ivy League credentials, if you didn't work at these places, if you don't have these connections, you have no shot at these roles."

But Ify flipped the script. And for that she's a visionary, point blank.

In my workplace, I've learned to follow more of that lead, and find my own flavor of it. Like how I think "visibility is a pathway to equity." Ify didn't say that, that's my tagline.

But in using her vision of how she sees the work, I've learned certain principles that have worked with the way that I believe the world moves, that, I believe, align with how she's built her firm.

●●••...•●

A visionary is someone who creates an idea or a business that no one else is doing, or very few are doing, right? They're able to connect dots in various ways.

Have you ever seen the exercise where there are nine dots on a page and you're told to connect them without lifting your pencil off the page?

Ify is the kind of person who would intuitively know to move outside of the nine dots in order to connect all of them. She sees patterns where others don't.

It's hard to catch Ify. I would say the one thing about the Visionary is that they're one of the hardest people to catch because they're in the clouds. They're ten years ahead of everybody else and it is hard to ground them and find time with them.

My experience with Ify is that when I get time with her, it's valuable. It's just about when I can do it. I was supposed to talk with her a couple of weeks ago, and then we went back and forth. I'd say, "hey, here's a time." but I do not hear back from her.

Sometimes the best way to get the time of the Visionary is to watch what they do. In your circle of champions the Visionary is not going to be the type of person, unlike the Empathetic Teacher and other folks, who is going to say, "hey, yeah, let's meet every two or three months." With visionaries, you gotta catch them when you catch them.

I have a call every two months to talk with Ify. I'm lucky if three of those happen. But I understand this is the nature of the relationship, because Ify keeps it moving. You catch her if you catch her. And then when we chat, sometimes it's a good hour and a half to an hour and 45. It's really funny, we stay in the clouds dreaming about what's possible. I like hearing what she's dreaming of and then it gets me dreaming about what's possible for me in my career.

You know, she's one of the many people who has said, "why are you not doing your book? You have so much brilliance to share. You're just like me. You're a visionary too." In my words, being a kid from New York City, "game recognizes game."

When we met in person in late 2013, early 2014, game recognize game. That's when there was this mutual admiration. The initial conversation went like, "you're Ron Rapatalo!", "You're Ify Walker!"

It was probably similar to when Jay Z and Nas finally met in person. I'm sure that happened somewhere in New York City in their early rapping days, with that level of, "I see you."

Technically, Ify is a competitor. I've lost some searches to her firm, but I don't see her as a competitor. I don't mind losing to her because I know that the work that she and her firm do is of the highest level and they have deep care for people of color in particular. I know she's going to push the needle on how clients think on equity.

In my experience, when you deal with a visionary you end up thinking, "damn."

It's like in basketball, LeBron is 38 and he now has "the thing". I don't want to say he is the only player to have done this, but I read this in Bleacher Report. He has scored 40 points against every team in the NBA. You know what kind of excellence he needed to have to do that? That's crazy.

That's Ify and search, that unparalleled excellence, being able to see ahead and create a structure where you demand excellence. That is really effing hard to pull off, to demand it every day, every minute. It's hard.

I aspire to be like that. I carry excellence in different ways. I aspire to be like that. I'm not exactly like that, but I'm not exactly far from it either. That's why I can hang with people like Ify, right? Ify doesn't have a lot of patience. Like any visionary, if you are not in that orbit, oh boy.

The Visionary is a very special person to get into your circle of champions. They are arguably the hardest person to find because they ain't going to have time for you if you're full of shit or if you are bullshitting – nah, they won't make time for you.

But if you can find them, they're a special person to have in your circle of champions.

●●•••●●

Ify knows talent when she sees it. It's hard for me to even describe how I do it. I can approximate it. You know, I think how Ify and I recognize game is through our ability to see people's strengths really fast. Like when you talk to someone, there could be a directness about them, and it doesn't always have to be really overt or strong. I think when you see that someone does really good work, you either know it by witnessing it, you hear other people talk about them or from the way that they talk about themselves.

There's this level of, "oh, yeah, you're it." It's not always candidates who hit the usual markers, because those are easy to use.

Our brains are conditioned to use proxies like, "Oh, Ron, you went to NYU, you were a neuroscience major, you went to Stuyvesant High School, you did Teach for America, right?"

No, it's a lot deeper than that. It's very much focused on one's values. For me, that's a big thing.

I think for me, the notion of 'game recognizing game' deeply comes in understanding that both Ify and I have values that allow folks to do really well in life. Working hard, being really generous, being able to connect the dots, being able to, on some level, do whatever it takes. Having deep care for people. There's all these things. It's like, when you talk to them, you can see that, right?

When I contrast that with the Manipulator I previously spoke about, they're willing to do whatever it takes, but they don't have deep care and empathy. They play a good game with it, with small talk. So you get some of the easy stuff, but I'm gonna be clear with you. I've had conversations recently with folks who work with the Manipulator and it corroborated that unfortunately the Manipulator, at least from the snippets I've gotten, hasn't really grown.

"Oh, this person's really struggling with equity. They don't really care about these things and the way they're managing..." I believe that when you want someone who has the values of what's enduring, and where people see you doing good work and they want to be around you, you're not only just doing whatever it takes, but you're going to do your work with care.

For me, the through-line of six of the seven people in the circle of champions is this empathy and deep care. Not to say I learned nothing from the Manipulator, because I did, but I question what they have in terms of deep care and empathy. There's varying levels of that and how it shows up and why, is based on how that person in the circle of champions moves and thinks.

●●●...●●

With the Visionary, it's a lot of "you see what you don't see" about your career. They can help you to pivot to things and explore things that you never thought were imaginable.

Yesterday, I was talking with a senior leader that I've been seeing around and she said, "you know what? One of the things that I wonder about is, how can we have project management certification start in K-12 education?"

In my experience, most people get their PMP post-undergrad, many years later. Now, I don't know what the hell is in the PMP cert off the top of my head, but if we are already teaching coding and the principles of software engineering in schools, then I'm not led to believe that its curriculum and coursework couldn't be done in high school.

With that leader's idea, I had like two observations. One, I didn't think I'd seen it done anywhere. Two, for me, the visionary thought was, 'I think you need to create this.'

I said, "my inclination is that I think you need to create it. If you're willing to create it, I think you're onto something."

When someone is passionate about something, it's easy to sometimes say, in my experience, "well, you just need to go to an employer to find that."

But no.

For me, the Visionary pushes you to think outside of the box of a full-time job. We have been conditioned so much in society to say, you have to just hop from job to job. I'm not saying there's anything wrong with that, but for me, the visionaries open up your aperture for what is possible. It might be switching sectors. It might be taking on different roles that allow you to leverage strengths.

People like me who recruit and do hiring really well can also do fundraising and marketing really well too. They're all country cousins of each other, that's what I like to call them. People say, "oh, if I've only recruited, I have to keep recruiting." To that I say, "no, that's not true."

Some of it is taking someone's discernible skill sets and passions and saying, "what are things that overlap?" When I think about how we as visionaries tend to think, it's like being able to see the concentric circles and overlaps pretty easily. That's what's different about the Visionary.

A lot of other people have to connect the dots of the concentric circles in order to do it. The way that visionaries work is with different size circles that tend to overlap.

I can just imagine it and just see a pattern. That's not everybody's skill set, right? Do I think you could teach it? At some level.

When I think about why I think I have that skill set, and why visionaries have that skill set, for me, one of the things that I studied was organic chemistry in college. There's this idea of stereochemistry. It's the study of the different spatial arrangements of atoms in molecules.

I forget why, but we used to have these models of molecules we would play with to be able to see their arrangements. Now, the way my brain works is I literally am able to take things in my head and I am able to see them without having to have something 2D right in front of me. I can flip things in my head.

Visionaries, I think, tend to have a similar skill of being able to take things and connect things that just don't really make sense in a 2D world. They are able to do things and connect and I think those are the really hard things to teach. I think there are ways you can get folks to learn to be creative, but when I think of someone like my friend Ify and I, as visionaries, there's a lot about our story that I think created the environment for us to nurture our vision.

If I didn't take organic chemistry, if I didn't have the rigor of the kinds of creative writing and history courses that I took, if I didn't have to lead at times with limited resources and get really creative to do the things that I've done, and the depth of people that I've gotten to know, I don't know if I'd have the same visionary skills.

I'm not the type to believe that visionaries all come out of the womb as a visionary. There's some level of nurture, and my belief about the visionary is they are someone who has the environment to build depth and breadth in their life, because at some level, when I think about my intuition, being a visionary is relatively similar. Like those things have to be nurtured. I have to be in environments where I can be able to utilize that skill set, because without it, it just doesn't magically turn on.

Look at Jay-Z's genius. I don't know if you know, Jay-Z has an almost photographic memory. He does not write his rap lyrics. I don't know another rapper that does that, that I've ever witnessed or heard about. All of the stuff he raps is in his effing head. Do you know how brilliant you have to be to be able to do that? Another anecdote that I learned is as a sixth-grade student, he scored a 12th grade level in reading.

Some people are just built differently. I'm a huge fan of Jay-Z, right? He had opportunities because the genius was equally distributed. The opportunity wasn't, and he found the opportunity. He made the opportunity, but he almost didn't have it. I think he's a visionary.

I think I've seen patterns of how visionaries think. It's just that there's something there, they see the world so differently, but if they don't get the opportunity, they are not able to manifest that genius.

Leader

For me, when I think of genius, when I think of a visionary, and particularly Ify, it's the way that she has been able to do her searches and be really focused.

Search, generally, for C-suite leaders, is something like a six month process. You have to do all these steps and all these things. It's like being on a reality dating show for six months.

It's all these steps and you're gathering all this stuff. You're taking all this evidence and all this documentation but, Ify's genius goes, 'wait a second, what's wrong with that process? Why does it take so long?' No one had questioned it in the way she did, from what I've watched.

It then became a case of asking, how do we compress it in a way where we're still getting the same evidence, in an express amount of time, but also allowing candidates to flourish and show their genius? Written exercises, video interviews, right? Allowing candidates to be able to learn about the full breadth of the role.

One of Ify's geniuses is the transparency that she models in her firm. This is, I think, the real genius, right? She has a FAQs document for most of the roles that are marketed when you want to work with her. Not everybody in search wants to be transparent in saying "here's what's good and bad and ugly about an organization, and we're going to let you as a candidate know that." We don't do it in Edgility yet.

No other firm that I know has public documents like that. If you go to OFFOR.co, if you look up some of the roles that are there and click on something, there's this FAQ document. There are questions that are asked of the client that are then put out in public, and people are asked, "what's something that someone needs to know, like what's an unwritten rule of working here? What's an unwritten rule of working with the manager?"

When are these things ever talked about? Never. That's genius, right? We're going to put it up on a tray for all of you. Not everybody wants to do that, nobody wants to pay the price point either.

But for me, if you want the really good stuff, then it is like going to Tiffany's versus going somewhere else to get your diamond ring. It's really expensive but it's a really high quality service. They're going to be so knowledgeable that they're going to push your thinking.

Not everybody wants that. That's the genius of what Ify's done for her firm that I've watched and learned about, because I also used to subcontract with her. So I know a little bit. The model, I'm sure, has evolved since I worked with her last in 2018. But for me, her genius was being able to take something and being able to connect dots in ways that no one else was willing to do.

Source Of Warmth

Do you know what warmth is?

I remember sitting down with Ify and it was almost like she turned her body towards me. I instantly said, "yeah, I'm struggling here at work."

And she replied, with this warmth, saying, "Ron," it was almost like there was this switch in energy and tone of like, "okay, Ron, what do you need?"

She asked me all these questions and then inspired me by saying, "what do you want to do next? And where do you see yourself? And wait, it sounds like you could be helping me because you're really good at the same stuff that my firm does. You're great with candidates. You're really warm. You have a strong equity mindset and you care about things that I care about."

You know, it could have been really easy for her to not do that. We were on the train and she could have said "oh, let me talk to you about this later." Instead, I mean, I almost thought she was going to come off at my train stop because she was living in Brooklyn at the time and from Newark, that's a good 15, 20 minute ride. It felt like that ride was an hour because of the level of focus and warmth she had with me.

The outcome of the conversation was that she said – let's figure out how to get you to work with me, as an offer, saying, "I got you." And granted, it was the first time that I'd met her and for her to say that, it was just astounding. It was like, 'wow.' For someone to offer that? That's not common.

It just goes back to "game recognizes game", right? She just knew it. She told me she had something for me and wanted us to figure it out.

●●•••●●

The nature of the Visionary is such that trying to catch them is akin to trying to catch a firefly. When you catch it, it's wonderful. I remember the last convo we had, and it's funny because when we do talk, it tends to be when Ify is taking a walk. We're chatting, we're multitasking, but I still feel the warmth over the phone when she says, "Ron, how are you doing? How's the family? How's your wife?"

She always asks me about my fitness. She tells me my fitness is crazy. That I often inspire her. She says, "Ron, you can always help me with that. Hold me accountable. And now, what are you doing? Let me learn from that."

What I always want to ask after we speak is, "what are you seeing in the space, Ify? What are you pushing? Where are you growing as a firm?"

Because I'm a senior leader, I'm learning from her about her vision and I want to ask -- "what are you seeing?" We get to just talk about those things. And so I get the warmth there too, because there's a warmth of generosity in her advice and wisdom.

Time spent with the Visionary, like when you catch the firefly and get it inside a container, is electric.

Confidant

When I was at a point where I knew I got demoted, I was told about my responsibilities and it felt very demeaning, I confided all that in Ify. I told her, "this is what happened." She replied with, "oh my God, I can't believe that happened to you, that is so not who I know who you are, who I believe you to be, and you deserve better."

For me to just hear that from someone that I had just started really getting to know, but whom I had a mutual deep admiration for already, was special. There are a lot of folks who will empathize, but not go beyond the, "Hey, I hear you."

There was a validation of my experience that was different from how other people show up in convos like that. Ify believed me. That's the key, right? Sometimes when you have convos like that, people say, "let me not say I believe you because for me to say that might be this leap of faith. What if you're not telling the truth?"

● ● ● ... ● ● ●

I've confided in Ify when thinking about what I want for my career. I know that I'm at my best when I do external work, public speaking, coaching people, selling, whenever I find my passions. Ify said, "Ron, I remember we've had conversations like this and if I ever can find a role for you where you do that for me, I would love to have you on my team."

You know, when I've talked in other conversations, there's this corroboration of things that I think Ify, as the Visionary, is really good at, because when you're matchmaking and talent brokering, you have to also hear how other people talk about people. That's part of the job, right?

It can't just be about a closed process and what "game" you talk about, because some people just talk a really good game. But then when you actually talk with people about their experiences of working with that person, you might find out they're actually an Manipulator. Manipulators are really coming into interview processes and feeling like they're the Empathetic Teacher. They can put on a mask.

You know, for Ify and I, where our brilliance comes in is in having our ears to the ground. Because people tell us a lot of things. We are the confidants, and we hear lots of things about people.

I always kid around that I'm like Edward Snowden. If I were to tell what I know about organizations and people that I've learned about, I'd have to leave the country. It's not always really good stuff that I hear about people in their work. My reply is, "oh my, what happened?" But I keep that stuff tight to a vest.

I had a conversation yesterday with someone that I placed. She said, "Ron, I knew I could trust you." I placed her some years ago, and before that this person confided in me, "this environment I work at is toxic, it's traumatic. I now have high blood pressure."

Ify does the same thing, she says to choose yourself. Don't kill yourself and backbreak doing this job. You can pick and choose. You deserve that, right? It's easy in those convos to say "oh, do the best that you can get." But no, I try to go a level or two deeper. This is where, for me, the No-Nonsense Nurturer comes in. You have to validate people in these conversations.

Advisor

Ify was my advisor around how executive search could be done more equitably, how we could push clients more on their equity journey. Because folks resist this work at some level, like my manager says at Edgility, "at times we're organizations' therapists." It's really hard work.

People confide in you and they tell you things and, oh my God, you have to have the energy and the wherewithal to show up for these convos. It's exhausting. I've gotten advice from Ify on how she's handled that. I've also gotten advice from Ify on how to advocate better for myself too. There's a little bit of the No-Nonsense Nurturer in the Visionary. With Ify, those are bundled together and I've gotten that advice from her too.

●●•••●●

When I was a solopreneur, I think Ify did that as a gift to me, the way she would pay me. She'd say, "Ron, I don't care if you get five candidates for me in this search in 5 hours or 50 hours. You get me the five, I pay you the money. You go off to the races."

So when I started to think about pricing for myself, one of the ways I had learned to price my value to clients was to think about it as a per-hour basis, like "here's the salary that you want, you add benefits to it as a consultant, so here's your total comp, your total value and money."

Then you break it down by 50 weeks. You get two weeks of vacation, you come up with a weekly rate. Maybe some people have an hourly rate, and there are some people that want to pay you an hourly rate. But you make better money when you charge a flat fee.

What I really learned from Ify, is to advocate better for the flat fee. Over time, I've just learned to advocate better for that. Not only when I was a solopreneur, but even inside of Edgility, I have learned that I sell better on the flat fee because I know the value that our work has.

When you can talk about the value and expertise you have, the number is just a number. I don't have any trepidation in saying, "yeah, what we cost is $70,000. It's expensive for the sector." Then people say, "oh, can you do that for $14,000?" I say, "no. If you find someone else who can do that for you, go ahead."

It's like the difference in saying I'm going to go get a dress in Target versus Barneys. Target may be what you need. I'm not mad at Target, I shop a lot at Target. Barneys, I think, is cool. It's since closed but this is the place you went to get really high fashion couture labels at a pretty pricey point. You know what you get when you're paying that.

I've learned to have confidence in my value through Ify. I don't think I had that as much until I started having those conversations with her, and now I share that with others because people ask me for advice. People ask, "how do you have that confidence?" I reply, "you should have met 35-year-old Ron."

Recognizes the Game

There was that moment of mutual admiration, when Ify and I first talked about those Delaware roles, she said "Marcus talks so well about you, Ron," It was this really nice voice that I really wish I could have kept. There was this warmth, there was this, "this is what I've heard about you."

Ify told me that another person that we knew through our Teach for America work, Christopher, spoke well of me. She was like, "I believe that. So I'm going to have a convo with you to explore these opportunities. I think this could be wonderful for you."

We talked, and I learned a little bit about it. I was willing to explore it, but it was like, "hell no, we're not going to Delaware." I was like, 'yeah, kibosh that,' right?

But, that was game recognizing game because, one, Ify shared what she had through other people we both had strong mutual relationships with. Two, she got it from talking with me and hearing a little bit about how I thought about what my experiences were. So then the ultimate game recognizes game moment was to hear her speak and for her to hear me speak at the Teach for America event in Newark.

We both think really similarly about how we advise people in their careers and what we value and why we do this work. It was almost like we were at the same hip hop concert and we both went one right after the other and kind of did our 30, 45 minute set. I replied with, "oh, damn, you know how to move a crowd. Your stories are really resonating with me."

We're both children of immigrants; she of Nigerian immigrants, I of Filipino immigrants. There were things in the way we grew up that weren't easy. There are lots of things we had to figure out and there are lots of things we had to unwind about how we learned and how we did things. There are things we learned to do better because of how we dreamed and what we thought was possible. Partly that came from our parents and our family and partly that came from us just being dreamers,

I think the thing about Ify that I just have admired is her daring to dream to be better and be better for others.

That's where you want a visionary in life. They're daring to dream and saying, you know, if you dream this, you really can get it. And sometimes people are scared to say their dreams out loud. Why? Because I think the belief of maybe failing to get that dream stops them.

For me, there's a level of fearlessness that I've learned from Ify. That, a lot, comes from the way we've lived. I've learned to be more fearless, the foundation of that is my parents. Their fearlessness got me to this country, with six of us. That's fearlessness, my God. Ify has a similar story, coming with her parents.

Sometimes you have the alchemy to be fearless because of the very people in your family that brought you here, and created the conditions for you to be even more fearless.

Visionaries have a level of fearlessness. When you dream like that, when you put it out there, what I've seen is that folks can be really afraid to say those things because one of the things I go back to that I've read over and over again and experienced again and again is that when I put the dream out and the direction, I don't worry about the outcome as much.

Do I wanna be a billionaire? Yeah, I'd like to be. That's the direction I wanna go in. The outcome of the billionaire is almost like this – if I ended up being a hundred millionaire, that's pretty damn good, right?

So for me, I dream to live a life where I work 20, 30 hours a week, and I'm traveling the world with my family, with multiple residences, impacting people, advising, coaching, having a Netflix show or something that follows us around, that pays us. I don't know how the hell I'm gonna get there, but I'm naming it. And will it exactly happen like that? I have no idea, but I feel it. I'm not afraid to say it.

And that's the thing about the advice of the visionary, when you name what you want, you have to be fearless about it, you name it. Because oftentimes when you name it, the energy of the universe and people, when they start to hear it, they conspire to get you there.

You have to be fearless, sometimes the direction to get you there is gonna have you uncomfortable. There's a level of uncomfortability that's gonna come with the ambiguity of not exactly knowing where you're gonna land. But if you're excited about the direction and the journey, that's the meta-advice of all of these folks in the circle of champions. You will always land on your feet. You'll be like a cat, right?

The Visionary and I, because I'm also a visionary, are fearless about it.

●●•••●●

When you think about people who are the folks on your LinkedIn and Facebook and Instagram who write about things where you end up thinking, "I'd never thought that before. I want to live my life in that way and I haven't yet said it. I want my career to be like that." It might be a visionary, who has written that.

It could also be the person who's quietly working, who just maybe is not saying it to everybody. They may not be on social media, and maybe they've got a big dream and they're just grinding at the moment. Some of it, frankly, is asking someone, "what do you dream to be?" You'll find out pretty quickly if someone's a visionary, because if you ask that question and someone doesn't have an answer, they're not yet a visionary. I think it's a pretty simple tell.

They're hard to find, but I think asking that question to figure out if someone's a visionary is, in my estimation, easy. If you ask me what my dream is, I got it. If someone hasn't formulated it, they're not there yet. It doesn't mean that they can't get there, but they're not the Visionary in your circle of champions. There's a clarity of thought that the Visionary has in telling you what they want. It doesn't mean they've gotten there, it just means they know where they want to go.

Ask about why they're daring to dream like that. What is it about their mindset, their life and their career that has them see that they want to be that? Then there's also the questions where you backwards map from that. How is that person thinking about the directions to get there?

I often think, I'd like to say by 50, if not earlier, I want to speak about my book, or run my podcast live at Madison Square Garden. If I think about that, I'm on stage doing it. I have my wireless mic, I feel the crowd. I see my wife and my daughters and the people that I love sitting in the front, and I'm starting to talk and I feel the energy in Madison Square Garden, I see the Knicks banner and other things. I'm realizing that this is where great sports events have happened, where great artists have come, great people have come, to talk and do things.

And people will say, "well how the fuck do I get there?" Well, do you see the stuff that I'm doing on social media? Y'all don't find me if I don't do all my content work on LinkedIn. I know how this game goes. Y'all do research on this shit. Y'all aren't going to come to me if I'm not on these things. Like who the fuck am I? My game recognizes your game, right?

And what advice you get from the Visionary, from me, is that I'm doing all the work that people can see, but there's also a lot of stuff that's unseen that you can learn from the Visionary that I don't even talk about. All the things people see with me being a visionary is the tip of the iceberg. I have 500 things that I do that spin people's wheels. They say, "how the fuck do you do so much in a day?" I reply with, "good habits, things that I know to do that are leveraging myself where I'm best, realizing this is a team effort, not only with my circle of champions but a hell of a lot of people that aren't even in this damn book."

That's what you learn from the Visionary, you might think they're in the clouds, but there's a lot of deeper thought beneath the tip of the iceberg. There's a lot about how we actualize it and how we're going to actualize the dream that directs us.

●●•...●●

I've learned to really assess clients more on where they are in their equity. Meaning, what are their mindsets around how they believe candidates should be coming into their process, but also what results have they had?

It's questions like, how many people of color are in leadership here? How many folks have you retained? What is your plan? What do you value? What's your self-awareness? What's your humility about these things?

At times I'd be afraid to ask those things early in my career because I didn't want to not get the business and not get paid. I have learned to be fearless in saying, for me, to do this work right, I have to be fearless about telling folks that they're just not right for me, and Edgility, because they don't align with our values.

I wanna work more and more with people who align with our values so that they can be better for the people that we place.

When you are fearless about that, people find you. I'll be clear, if I showed you all, I got receipts. People find me all the time. People refer me. It's a real deep blessing, and I talk to people about the things that people don't see, that I do, every day. I probably had five to six convos like that today, advising people who are senior leaders.

Ify does a very similar thing. People ask her for advice all the time like that. I talk about that at some level, but it's very much below the tip of the iceberg, right? That allows me to be able to be generous and build relationships with people because those folks will evangelize me in the work that I do at Edgility and therefore bring more people in for the work that we do.

It's a lot of my "je ne sais quoi." It's the stuff where I think my reputation precedes me, and the pattern happens over and over again, because if all I did was "talk a good game" on social media, I don't know if I'd have the same deep reputation. I do the work on Zoom and phone convos to build relationships and give advice to people.

When I write a second book about all the career advice nuggets I've shared with people, shit, that shit will be a bestseller. I have no doubt. God's honest truth, the shit that I say, it's like I'm a jazz musician; I feel like John Coltrane.

I don't even know what I'm going to say 90% of the time. But when I'm in the context of the flow, it's like—how the hell did the song, 'So what,' happen? How did Coltrane do all of his riffs? How did he do 'Love Supreme?' I don't know how I do what I do, but when I tell you the stories, you'll start to piece it together. I know that visionaries like myself and Ify do that really well. Cause I learned how she does it. I go, "oh, damn, there's a lot here."

Visionaries, when they can actualize their vision, are a lot more structured than you think. People don't think that I'm structured. I think by design, I've kind of told myself I'm not a really structured person. I'm realizing more and more that that's a lie.

I've learned that when I have a structure I believe I'm unstoppable. Or a phrase that I like to use, I'm "RON-stoppable." Get it?

Like my workout program, when I'm coming off a workout and I'm in the program that I'm doing with my barbell training, I tell the trainers, "I'm really seeing the results. I'm seeing the way my body feels and how the weights I move feel lighter." It is crazy to think about.

I'll give you an example, tomorrow I have to squat 310 pounds. It's almost two times my body weight. I'm about a buck 85, buck 90, right? I have to deadlift about 335 pounds for my program, right? But it's not the number, it's my technique. It's the work that I do. It's all the stuff, like I'm in a really good structure.

When you put a visionary like me in a really good structure, I think, 'I know I could do that.' It's because I've had enough results, but I'm not there yet. I've seen folks that lift 800 pounds. Now, do I aspire to deadlift 800 pounds? No. My aspiration is to probably do 550, 600 pounds. I want to do three times my body weight, assuming that I'll get bigger.

So why do I say those things? Because when you work with a visionary there's a lot more you can get from your thoughts, and the details matter.

●●•••●●

Ify, thank you for having me dream bigger and be more confident about my value. Thank you for having me be able to push more on clients about how to be more equitable to candidates of color and to advocate for people of color, because we're not often in the room.

And thank you for seeing a part of myself that I was afraid to actualize.

CHAPTER SEVEN

Personal Sage
– Shanita

In a world filled with shallow facades and too many distractions, finding a Personal Sage can make all the difference. They are someone who can guide you through difficult conversations, create a safe and nurturing space for you to give and receive feedback and offer valuable insights without ever making you question their intentions.

I think you have to reach a point in your life where you have other people reflect the mirror back on you in a way that is genuinely caring and nurturing so you can grow and build your life. It's like a Venn Diagram where one circle represents what you know, another circle represents what you know you don't know, and the third circle represents what you don't know, you don't know.

To be ready for the Personal Sage, you need to first have met the six other champions of your circle.

You need to build your muscles for deeper self-awareness of what you know you know and what you know you don't know. You're only ready for the Personal Sage and for the "what you don't know, you don't know," if you have already started playing with those two other circles of the Venn Diagram. If you haven't, you're just going to get upset and you're not going to want to hear what they say.

My wife Shanita belongs to "what you don't know, you don't know." She has the ability to say, "Hey, here are some things that I'm going to share with you that I don't think you are aware of, and because we have this deep, trusting, and loving relationship, I'm going to tell you these things." It's a shock to the system, but in a nurtured relationship, you can uncover your patterns in a loving way.

The concept of an Empathetic Teacher comes full circle when you consider the role of a Personal Sage. An Empathetic Teacher is like, "Ron, I need you to discover things about yourself, what you don't even know about yourself at this age." A Personal Sage, on the other hand, is like, "You know a lot about your stuff, but do you know what you don't know."

There is an intersection of how these concepts intersect with my career and family. One of the things I learned from Shanita is that I never really had a close relationship with my family. And one of the reasons I married her is because of how close she is with her own family. It was fascinating to me.

Due to the different traumas I dealt with in my family, I have never had the kind of close relationship with them that I see my wife have with her own family. I love them, but I get envious of my wife's "ride or die" relationship with her family.

I needed to learn from her how deeply important family is, and not only those related to her by blood. Her sorority sisters and her close friends whom she started teaching with in the 2000s are considered her family too. She's got some real rocks in her world.

Both of my daughters have Shanita's parents and uncle as godparents but none of my family and relatives hold that role. I have a loving family, don't get me wrong, but there is certainly a contrast in relationship dynamics. I learned from Shanita the value of family, not just by blood but of people you love and care about deeply. She helped me appreciate what it means to act with genuine connection and understanding that enables me to work with others. Family means the people you love and care about unconditionally and vice versa.

Shanita and I were just talking recently in the car about how my sense of direction needs a frame of reference before I learn. This was an uncovering. I don't usually get anxious and when I do, it's only when I am in a state of learning and I don't have a frame of reference. As we were dropping off our girls, I uncovered this for the first time in that car ride. Shanita was like, "yeah, you don't do well with that." She was right. When I have a frame of reference or a framework, I feel really comfortable learning and doing whatever I need to do, and if I don't, I get really anxious.

We were talking about how easily I get lost. She, on the other hand, doesn't panic. We talked about where anxiety starts and how it originates from not knowing. Shanita deals with ambiguity quite comfortably. She doesn't need to always have a frame of reference and she will just figure it out.

I am nothing like that and that is such a therapeutic confession. My adaptive mechanism has always been to find the frame of reference. When looking for directions, I have to memorize where I'm going. And even then, every once in a while, if my frame of reference gets reoriented and I'm going in the opposite direction, I will somewhat panic. It sounds crazy but I will be walking around a neighborhood and be like, "where the hell am

I?" Shanita's like, "Rob, you know the street after this because we're just coming from a different angle." I'm like, "Ooooh," I just switched it up in my head.

Shanita's anchor has always been her family and I learned things from my family as a frame of reference. The paths have been different, but the lessons have been very similar.

As for me, she's my number one.

My "ride or die."

● ● ● ... ● ●

A Personal Sage, for me, is someone who puts up a mirror and shows you all the things that you have no idea that are going on with you. And they don't just help you deal with it, but they also cut through the bullshit.

When I struggled with my career, like being fired the first time, or having "quiet firing" happen to me a second time, my Personal Sage was one of the first people I went to talk to about how I was feeling.

Shanita was a Personal Sage for me when all of that was going on. I showed her the final written warning to me. I got informal things like, "Hey, Ron, your performance sucks, you're now in a PIP (Performance Improvement

Plan)," just three weeks after I started the job. It was a tough time and I was processing all of it with her.

Part of me wanted to fight and say, "This is cognitively dissonant from who I am." When I showed it to her, she said, "Ron, they don't want you. You don't see that?" The truth is, I felt it, but I didn't want to admit it because in my world everybody loves Ron Rapatalo.

That time, she was able to say, "this letter and what you shared with me about them, they don't want you. Why are you fighting this?" I admit that I was being stubborn about it and there have been many times that I was stubborn to Shanita's advice. Sometimes, I still am. But she is often right.

I could have just quit the job back then, rather than sit around for two weeks in a daze. But I needed to go through that. When I left and I got the letter, she was like, "Ron, you know everybody loves you, right? Reach out to those people. They're going to take care of you. I'm going to take care of you." Three weeks later I landed a year-long consulting project. Shanita was, once again, right. And that is why, through all those struggles, she was my Personal Sage. She was there for me to say "Let me cut through all this stuff. You're holding on to something that's just not there."

● ● ● ● ● ● ● ●

A Personal Sage is willing to cut through the bullshit. They are nurturing, loving and deeply empathetic.

The feeling I get with a Personal Sage is that it's someone who is able to hold your fear and anxiety and embrace it in a way that makes you feel safe to examine those things.

They recognize patterns. They have a depth and breadth of context acquired through their own experience and they are able to share that experience with others as lessons or pieces of advice through relatable stories and anecdotes. They just can pull from so many things. That might be part of pattern recognition, frankly.

But one thing is clear. They will do anything for you any time any day. It might be easier said than done but that is the feeling I get.

Give Safety

Safety can sometimes be found in silence, especially after a really long day at work. We decided to make this a priority so we put it on our calendar, at least four times a week. We are both executives at work and we both have busy schedules as a married couple. We also recently went to couples therapy just to hash some things out. At this point in our lives, we both feel secure and comfortable holding and creating a space for each other which is so important.

It is in this space of silence, while we're having tea and cookies and watching Meghan and Harry on Netflix, that we allow a certain level of ourselves to simply let go and take our minds off work after an exhausting day.

Shanita deals with school-related matters at work. I handle organizational decisions that come with holding a lot of emotional weight for team members who are transitioning out. That space we hold for each other is where we can relax while talking about Meghan and Harry and the royal family. We can be authentic with ourselves instead of presenting composure because we have to lead others at work. You can't always put yourself in front of people.

Shanita is a mother, a daughter, and a national literacy leader. She is an introvert and is like a quiet simmering boil. She is a beautiful Black woman and she's very loyal. She's also guarded, but once you get into her cocoon, she's like a good, warm, chocolate souffle. She's always had this deep, affectionate side to her but she is careful who to let in. This is why she's the right Personal Sage for me, our energies complement each other perfectly. If I had someone that acted like me as my Personal Sage, it just wouldn't work.

After I was fired from my last job, I had fear and anxiety about finding the next job despite projecting confidence publicly. I'd say, "I'm going to figure it out." But inside, I was really worried because we had just been married a couple of years, we were about to have a baby girl and I didn't have a job. At the time, we were living in an expensive one-bedroom apartment on the Upper West Side, and unemployment benefits only covered so much. I was the provider and the protector, and with no job I couldn't fulfill those roles anymore. But Shanita said, "Ron, we will figure it out. I can provide, do what you need to do. I got us. It doesn't have to all be on you."

From a young age, I have always had this feeling of being overly personally responsible for everything. It's like I have been built this way. Watching my parents, and hearing their stories, I learned to just make shit happen. But in my relationship and marriage with Shanita, and her as my Personal Sage, we are a team. She made me feel that I didn't have to do everything myself. She created a safe space for me to say, "There are things I'm not as good at doing."

As a cis hetero male, that was hard to take and tell to someone. I was never conditioned to believe that. It was like "Ron, you just do it, you're a man. Man up." A lot of the wisdom I gained from working with Shanita as my Personal Sage is about embracing my vulnerability. I have always had it but I was afraid to show it. That's where the safety comes from. It is being able to say, "Actually, my strength has been my vulnerability."

She said that to me two days ago. We went around our leadership team table at a WeWork in Grand Central to give praise to each other. I received compliments from our leadership team members, including our two co-founders. They were like "Ron, people trust you. You're so vulnerable. People feel that." But I know I wouldn't have that without my 12 years of marriage to Shanita. It's a foundation that we've built and worked hard to deepen over the years.

Avoiding was one of the things I had learned to do well as an adaptive mechanism. At a young age, there were a lot of family fights. Especially among my two oldest siblings, my two brothers. There were times it became violent, and my oldest brother was pulling out the kitchen knife. This happened way too many times. He had violent tendencies, even on special, happy occasions. I remember on one of my dad's birthdays he didn't get what he wanted from my parents. He broke plates and threw my dad's birthday cake on the floor. I remember this. I was 9-years-old when this was happening.

I remember feeling unsafe because my family didn't talk about it. They were just like, "Oh, no, he is who he is." There were a lot of placations.

It was a stark contrast to how Shanita is. She will confront things if needed but she was very understanding in a, "she's lived through what she's lived through" way. She is like, "you can't just let that hang and push it out," which has been my tendency for so long.

A lot of my courage has come from seeing her example of how she is fearless in handling difficult conversations, not only at work but also with family, and she has coached me on this. There has been something truly beautiful about that process. I've always known I struggled with avoidance but during a recent therapy session, I became more open to receiving her information.

It is funny how life comes full circle. I saw my brother in Tampa. He used to be an Army Captain, so he was virile and physically strong before but now he is struggling to walk. He is the most virile brother that I had. He was both athletic and strong but now has arthritis in his knees and a limp. It was disconcerting to see my brother like that.

I saw the dynamic with him and his wife and I was taking this all in. I know his wife is trying to help him. I then processed this with Shanita and reflected on my own relationship. I know there are things I am still actively trying to get better at. One of them has been about avoidance, and us just having really tough and hard conversations which translate then to me being able to do that.

I got a call from a client today. She said, "Hey, Ron, I just wanted to share this dynamic I saw between your assistant and one of your colleagues. It seems like your assistant is being snippy with your colleague and I don't know if you knew." I thought, 'Ah, I need to talk to my assistant.' I can discuss this with him and we can unpack it together.

Five years ago, I would have been like 'I don't want him to not like me.' But that's what I have learned about having these kinds of conversations. You can have a tough conversation and still have it come from a place of love. It sounds corny. It's like, "I want you to get better because I love you." When I learned that, I was like, 'well, shit.'

Walking into those kinds of conversations, I might stumble on my words, it might not be perfect but when people know your intent, you get a lot more grace.

That's what I learned from Shanita and it has now become a superpower. People come to me left and right like, "Can we talk?" It's a weight, but it's also a weight that I have been building up to this whole time. I just have it now.

Shanita, you love me because you see through me and support me through my bullshit.

Cut Through The Bullshit

Deb Lang gives you information like it's a shot of tequila – with no chaser. There's always a valuable role for someone to say something unfiltered. Deb has been like that for me. It's a good counterbalance to my Personal Sage, Shanita, with whom I have a loving and caring relationship.

Even when we have our own trepidation and concerns, we still have moments where we hesitate because we don't want to hurt someone else's feelings. But Deb gives her unfiltered perspective. She will tell you the things you need to hear without sugar coating them. And it's not always going to feel good when you hear, "this is what you fucking need." I can almost hear her Chicago accent in my head, to tell me, "Ron, no, this is what you fucking need to do. Just do it. Stop, stop, stop that shit. Do this."

As I said earlier in the book, one of the big pieces of advice that Deb gave me went like, "You're in your 40s, a young man," Deb is in her 60s, if not 70s. These are your big years, Ron. It's not your 30s, it's your 40s. You want to be able to bank whatever that wealth is so when you get into your mid-50s, you have different decisions to make about how you want to have an impact and how you want to live your life. This is the time."

I had been thinking about writing a book and creating a podcast for some time but I always delayed it because I was waiting for the right timing. So, those words from Deb deeply resonated with me and instilled a sense of fear that made me question if I was doing enough. Deep down, I knew I wasn't.

I remember her telling me that, and I was like, "Oh shit." I have never had someone give advice like that. And it took Deb, the Straight Shooter with no tolerance for bullshit, and a wise, old soul.

This is where the Personal Sage and the Straight Shooter overlap. In some ways, Deb has Personal Sage qualities but her style is to motivate me to figure things out for myself. The Personal Sage, on the other hand, also gives me a sense of security while cutting through the bullshit.

●●••…••●

I have a tendency to tune out when I'm tired, which is not really a good trait.

I have an intense load of work and sometimes when I'm around Shanita, my girls and her family, I tune out to create a space for me. I get back into patterns of being selfish. Shanita has sent me many a-note at times when she has been really frustrated like "Ron, I was doing everything for the girls while we were here. You're not really engaged with us and the family, what the fuck is going on?"

The way she cut through the bullshit is like, "You know what? I love you, I care about you. And you know your girls and I need your help. The family wants to engage with you a bit more. They are not going to say anything to you, but I see it. So I'm going to tell you, I'm going to cut through all this stuff."

The advice she gave me that really cut through the bullshit, however, was during a couples therapy session. She said, "You know the Ron Rapatalo that I hear about from everyone else? I just want some of that at home. I'm not saying I need it all the time but I want some of that Ron too."

It suddenly dawned on me. I had turned that Ron off and I had to agree with her point. That's what I needed to hear. That was Shanita cutting through the bullshit.

Recognize The Patterns

Shanita just sees these patterns in me that maybe others don't.

As the youngest of seven children, I was raised self-centered and spoiled. I got everything, I was spoiled. As an only child, Shanita had to figure a lot of stuff out.

Even though both of us came from a big family, she had a different family dynamic. There was a different level of having to make things happen for her, because it was just her, even though she had people around.

I, on the other hand, had this big family that was all about catering to me. It was always about me and she has seen that pattern in me over and over again. Whether it's how I order food, or how I create my gym schedule without us talking. Now that we've had inter-ventions, we talk every week about our schedule, move things around and accommodate each other because marriage is no longer just about me, it's about both of us.

To this day, she is still seeing remnants of those patterns and it has been a continued unlearning for me because it's easy for me to get into my "deep frost" state. It's the Ron Show. Everybody loves Ron. So does Ron.

This lesson has translated so much to work and I give the same advice to people I meet. When I'm at work I center around the needs of others. I built a good culture of trust with the five people on my team because I center their needs.

I would be a bad manager if It was me first, you second. I have learned so much from my own dynamic and having a Personal Sage that cares and nurtures me has allowed me to grow. This sounds very Tony Robbins-esque like, "To get to really know how you're going to be as a person, you have to look at your parent dynamic."

There is a lot of wisdom I have gleaned through all the conversations I've had with Shanita, especially those related to our marriage. We spoke a lot about understanding our parent dynamics, and how we show up in our marriage, as parents to our kids, and at work.

It may bring about all your worst fears and anxiety, but for me, it was one of the most powerful things one can do. You are forced to face a lot of imperfections and no one likes to talk about the things you don't do well. I believe our brains are very much wired to not want to look at those things. Then our society doubles down like, "Keep it good! Don't worry!"

I'm quite aware that much of the trauma that affected my family stems from mental health issues, whether diagnosed or undiagnosed. It is a deep-seated problem we have that no one really likes to talk about, but my wife has talked about it with me. She's got it on her side too. This is not just a problem in American society, this is happening globally.

To understand my vulnerability, I had to understand that there has been a pattern of it in my own family, and understanding that pattern helped me to be better for myself, my family, my work and other people.

While I have my own struggles, I understand that I don't carry the same things that my fifth oldest brother does, who has been bipolar for 20 years. I don't even know where he is right now if I'm being honest. Somewhere in Queens. I have not talked to him in a year and a half.

I recognize that without this big cushion of amazing people to hold me, things could have turned out differently for me. I am aware of that now that I can see my own circle of champions. This circle of trust is a confluence of good luck, vision and people seeing the best of me.

But I have six other siblings whose lives are very different from the way that I live. Reflecting on all these differences and delving deeper into my personal experiences allows me to discuss these topics more openly.

Honestly, if I had done this 10 years ago, before I had Shanita, I wouldn't have had the wisdom, the deeper self-awareness, the vulnerability, and the lived experience to be able to come to you all and share these things.

Share Stories And Relate

Shanita shared with me a powerful story about her reconciliation with her father years ago. This is not really my story so I want to be careful how I share it but I can talk about it from a top level. What I have learned is that not only my own stories, but stories of others too, are important for my personal growth.

What I learned from how Shanita tried to re-establish and deepen her relationship with her father is that when you have an impasse with someone, you need to set up a space to give and receive feedback. The honest truth is, I think if she didn't have that conversation with her dad and started to lighten her load of how she sees herself in her relationships with men, I don't know if we would have found each other and gotten married.

The lesson is this: Sometimes you have to really dig deep and have those tough conversations, especially with the people that you love. There will be difficult times and you have to approach people with care.

How does this show up for me in the workplace? I make the decision to have courageous conversations with love. This is an exact quote from my manager: she said, "Ron, you approach me with things I may not want to hear, things I'm not aware of, with a level of care and courage." I said, "Do you know who I learned that from? Shanita."

When approaching difficult conversations now, I find that coming from a place of care makes it easier to use the tools and mechanisms to have productive discussions. But if I'm coming at it like, "I need to prove to you that you're wrong," it usually leads to a negative outcome. Your intent matters. That's the point.

When reconciling with her father, Shanita's intent was like, "I need to figure this out. I love my dad, so how do we make this better? How do I understand?"

That was the most important lesson for me and that's how I try to approach conversations ever since.

●●•••●●

If Shanita and I were recorded watching our Netflix shows, we'd probably have a great podcast by now. We watched episode four of Meghan and Harry, they're an hour long and we started watching at 9:30 in the evening so we were both exhausted and barely got an episode out. But this one was about their big marriage.

I remember the hubbub about it. Shanita is a big fan of British royalty, so she watched the whole damn thing. I watched bits and pieces of it until I became curious about the story. You have this biracial Black woman who was marrying into the royal family. It's really interesting. It then became a conversation about how Blackness is seen and heard not only in Britain but around the world.

We just started having these conversations about what she deals with as a Black woman and how I have tried to show up and support Black women. For me, a lot of our conversation about the show turned into talking about, not just the personal dynamic, but understanding the system and the history.

Shanita does equity work in a different way than I do. She does it in school and does it around instruction, like how to help school leaders. She comes in with a systemic approach for school systems to be able to ensure that kids have better academic and life outcomes. I'm approaching equity from the perspective of how to get folks to create a hiring process and place a leader.

The analysis that she and I had, which was interesting, was that perhaps people don't understand the system. Maybe they don't know about the brutality of British royalty and the commonwealth and what it did in India and Jamaica where slavery persisted and they still profited off the trade even after it was abolished by Britain in the 1830s.

Fast forward to today, the British media and their obsession with British royalty essentially has a lot to do with money. Shanita and I share this view that we can't look at the marriage of Harry and Meghan in isolation, as just about how they loved each other and how it's going to flourish. People are saying this is going to change how people see British royalty and the royal family will change.

On the individual level, change is hard. But on the systems level? Imagine that individual level but bubbled up with lots of other things. There was this "aha moment" when we talked, like, "this is why our work is so damn hard." We had this "oh shit" moment and then we could talk about things more openly, All from watching what looks like the marriage of marriages.

The Duchess was not fitting into how folks wanted to see a royal princess so Meghan and Harry started to get a lot more attention and it started cutting them at the knees like, "Meghan's being a diva." There are so many things coming out and most of it is untrue.

But also some of it was being leaked because each of the British royal members had their own communications house, which I thought was really fascinating. They snipe at each other by design. Part of what we were watching was Harry talking to his brother about how there was a commitment to not do that because they saw the strain that it had on their dad, Prince Charles, and their mom, Princess Diana.

It was all the more disappointing for him to see his brother doing it because one can make a reasonable argument that it was the British paparazzi that got Princess Diana killed.

They'll Do Anything For You

What Shanita and I have in common with Meghan and Harry, is a deep commitment to serving others. It's a beautiful similarity to what I think Harry learned from his Mom.

There was this story of Meghan in an African country, just being of service. Shanita and I have that same deep commitment to service.

The reason why there is a sense of safety in having Shanita as my Personal Sage is because of our deep shared commitment to serving others. I know what her intentions are 99% of the time and I trust her. You need someone in your life whose intent you never question. That's really hard to find but once you find it, everything else you hear, and don't want to hear, becomes a little bit easier.

You still have to learn some tools and strategies, but the headline is this: find someone whose intent you don't question and keep nurturing it with love and care. Even though I know we are going to continue to have difficult conversations at times, I don't ever question the intent of my Personal Sage.

In the patterns of divorce or why people leave jobs, one of the reasons people leave is because they begin to question the intent. Once that trust is eroded, it's really hard to recover from that.

●●●...●●

Here's a really funny story.

We had just gotten married, and I got really sick.

One of the things that I laugh about is the moment when I learned this term from the world of gender expression, 'a gestational parent,' but I'll say 'a mom.' When a woman gives birth, a gestational parent gives birth. And it's like going through a car crash. The immense pain that a gestational parent goes through is up the wazoo.

So I caught a stomach virus, and I was retching and shouting like I was in labor. This was early in our marriage so Shanita literally dropped everything to take care of me. Soup, shopping, compresses, and all the other errands. She did it all.

We laughed about it today. She tells me, "You were so dramatic, but I couldn't tell you that at that moment because you would have gotten really upset."

She simply had to nurture me back to health and as soon as I was feeling better, she would teasingly remind me about how I saw her give birth and have 36 hours of labor. Everyone has a different pain threshold, but looking back, I laugh about it because my stomach ache was no match for her experience.

That's how I know how far she would go and do anything for me, because she selflessly cared for me when I was at my weakest, physically. She dropped everything.

Not everyone's willing to do that, especially when you're vomiting and you smell. This is what they mean when they say "for better or for worse" in marriage vows.

●●•••●●

Everyone needs a Personal Sage. Find the one person whose intent you never question. The person who loves you without question. That's the first thing.

And the second thing is to create space, and consistent space, to share with each other, learn from each other and experience joy together, but also to have conversations when things aren't going well. Don't let the silence and the tension manifest into something that is harder to unpack.

So build your self-awareness around what you do well and what you don't know well. I think that's foundational. To be ready for the Personal Sage, you better have a good idea of how they will challenge you. Because otherwise, you're not going to be ready for when they start throwing shit at you.

You're going to be like, "Wait, what do you mean?" But they're going to do it like a "warm chocolate souffle" and you'll think 'I know that's going to get me to be better.'

But you can't get into the process of self-improvement without someone whose intent you don't question. That's a different level of relationship. You have to have the other experiences with your circle of champions to be ready for the Personal Sage.

Find yourself by talking to others that you believe know you and learn how they are seeing you. I think by the time you're getting ready for champion number seven, you need to have the courage to talk to others who just have a good sense of you. So it's about leveraging the other six on your journey.

I had these conversations years ago and I learned to know how others perceive me. Compliments are good when you hear them but what about when they talk about the things I'm not good at? What is something you think I don't know that I should get better at? You ask them questions and your role at that moment is to listen and capture their feedback, clarify and not get defensive. Then you take action. You ask yourself, 'What's one thing here, not 20, but one, that I could start acting on?'

When I think about this energetically, if you haven't already attracted that person into your life you're certainly gonna be more receptive to them.

$$\bullet\bullet\bullet\cdots\bullet\bullet\bullet$$

Shanita, our love, courage, and support for each other live through the beauty, wisdom, and curiosity of our two daughters.

Thank you for that gift.

Conclusion

We are creators.

We are all the visionaries of our lives.

But there's a lot of difficulty about the way that our lives are constructed. There's a lot of shit, there's a lot of challenges, there's a lot of anxiety, there's a lot of things holding us back. All of those things can be true, but focusing on our ability to create with and through others is the gift that we have as we live here on Earth.

When you do that, I go back to one of my favorite phrases, "what you intend, you manifest."

You can construct your life and your career as you dream it to be, but you need to do that with a circle of champions that's behind you every step of the way.

That circle of champions won't always be the same people. People come in and out of your life, but they don't ever leave you. They may leave you in the short term, but their lessons and their being never leave.

The gifts of these people are accessible in everyone's lives, and it's important to be a lot more conscious of how you're leveraging these people. I've developed a level of consciousness to how I got advice and support from the people I've leveraged. So in a lot of ways, this book is me telling seven stories of people who have impacted me greatly.

This is like my Love Opus, a love story to people who have given me the support, resources and advice I needed to be where I am today. I have this eternal gratitude for my champions and I want to share the lessons and stories that I've learned from them.

My strong hope is that reading these stories about these amazing people will lead to you realizing that you have similar stories with people in your own life, and reflecting on whether you've formally created a circle of champions or not.

You might think, 'wait a second, I had something like that happen to me in college,' or 'I had something like that happen to me yesterday,' or 'wait a second. I didn't think about that person being a Straight Shooter, but I should continue to reach out to them.'

I want to help my readers realize that the greatness of the people around them is theirs for the leveraging.

● ● ● ● ● ● ● ●

I had lunch with the Straight Shooter recently, and we were just catching up on life. She shared how she gives feedback to people.

She told me, "you know, Ron, I'm always firm, but I'm nice. People don't have to agree with me, but I just like to tell them what I see."

I started laughing.

I said to her, "you know, Deb, I have to fast forward. I wanted to tell you that you're in my book, and that advice? It's exactly what I talked about with you."

She smiled. It was an unspoken way of telling me, "Ron, that's who I am." Thinking about these stories and then having the opportunity to tell people they're in this book was a deepening point in my relationships with them.

People are willing to go to bat for you more when you deepen your relationship with them, whether it's for your career or your personal life.

Deb sent me this really nice text message after, "I'm so proud of the man that you've grown up to be." Because she's known me since 2005. There was something really nice about that statement. It was just like a mom being proud of me.

There was this moment of realizing that there are people in your life, the circle of champions, who also gain something deep while they're giving you advice.

I've realized that I'm in other people's circle of champions too. They are writing stories and things about me and vice versa. I just think there's so many lessons and values to be shared.

I'm involved in people's careers like that, which is really special to me.

●●●●●●●●

I probably fall most into being the Personal Sage, but I think I have a little bit of the Empathetic Teacher too. I can straight shoot, but that's not my default. I've learned to embrace that, as appropriate to the relationship I have with someone.

But I think I'm more of a combination of the bookends of this book, the Personal Sage and the Empathetic Teacher. I think my nature of wanting to listen, to ask questions, to provide advice and wisdom, that's my best energy.

When you listen to people, you can empathize and believe that what they're sharing with you has actually happened. I've seen that people don't believe their own stories when they share them.

It's not that you get access to the resources and the advice of someone and then you have the relationship, it's actually the reverse. You have to have the relationship and the trust-building first, and then all this other stuff happens and it deepens over time.

When you have relationships with people and you can hear folks' stories and you get their lessons, then you get access to all the other things.

As you're navigating your career, you need to be good to people and get to know them, but you also have to understand what you need.

Like I said earlier in this book, one of my favorite phrases is, "how do you unlock the natural propensity of people to be generous?" I found all seven of the archetypes of the folks in my circle of champions, that's what I did, and that's what they did for me.

The idea of generosity and relationships is non-negotiable when you're trying to find these people. Folks drop off if they feel like you're not being generous and they don't have a good and beneficial relationship with you. It's human nature.

You have to get something out of it. Even the most generous people, even me. You gotta get something out of it. Something. Feeling good. Feeling like you're giving advice. Seeing someone's growth. But you wouldn't have that sustainable circle with champions without building relationships first.

Ultimately, you don't have one person who sits in these roles in your entire life. While there are people who can play multiple roles, you just want some amalgamation of these types of people in your life in order to have the full benefit of opinion, advice, resources and trust.

●●●...●●

I have always had a thirst for learning from a young age. That has evolved to learning through others and with others.

You won't get a circle of champions if you think that you can learn on your own or that you can just read a book about it. I hope nobody reads this book and thinks, "I figured it out! I got it!" The value of learning with and through others is essential.

There is wisdom and knowledge from others that will compliment and push your thinking. You can't believe that you know it all. I used to, at some level, but there's just some things I don't know well, or as well as other people.

Leveraging those people becomes important to get a better 360° of what is going on in your world.

The ability to learn to listen to others and hear their stories is the other part. It has to go two ways. It can't just be "I'm doing these things, I'm getting, getting, getting, getting." In all of these relationships, it's about, at some level, starting to almost do the same thing.

When you start this practice of being the person who's being given advice at some level, then you are always learning. You hear the questions that they're asking you and at some level, you start to ask those questions yourself. It starts to deepen your understanding of what makes them tick. How did they come to be? What did they learn?

Some of that comes through the very nature of these relationships. People tell you things so you can learn from them. A lot of what I've learned from these really good relationships I've had is the very way that people question or listen or think. I picked these things up, and they are then what I use with others.

The third important value to have is this deep belief in the potential of others to be great. A number of my friends have said this, like Ify, who I talked about in this book.

She says this a lot, "Genius is equally distributed, opportunity is not." And at some level, relationships, like this idea of social capital, can equalize the playing field for people. I'm really bullish on the idea that when you get in front of people who can help you, it does things for your career and your life that can accelerate you in ways you had no idea were possible.

You know how they say "it takes a village to raise a child," or, "no one does it on their own" or all these things. I believe that to be true. There's no such thing as doing it on your own. Like if you look at any big entrepreneur or a celebrity, they didn't do it on their own. What fascinates me are those who hit it big 30-40 years into their career. What was their story?

Reading Steve Jobs' biography and getting his backstory is more instructive than the results he had, because you learn from the journey more than you do from results.

I couldn't have done it without Mr. Seluga being an equity champion and having my back after I talked to the folks from the school who had thought that I was white or Italian by my last name. They didn't really want to talk to me about that magnet middle school. I couldn't do it alone then because I didn't know exactly what was going on. I knew something was wrong.

I couldn't have done it without Mr. Irgang. He wrote me an incredible college recommendation. What was more important was his belief in me, his understanding of my Philippine culture and also his deepening of my critical thinking to understand American history and economics. I never could have done that on my own, and so he pushed me to do that.

With Allen, he had this ability to just understand my career arc from when I was just an undergrad. Then, to looking at the jobs boards and looking for student worker jobs, to being more involved on campus, to being a more involved alum and fighting more for diversity, equity, inclusion on campus. I couldn't have done that without Allen and the advice he gave me about how to navigate the university.

Allen also connected me to people. He still does it to this day. He's always connecting me with people, "hey, Ron, this person's looking, can you help them?" Now I'm the Career Yoda because he's pushing people my way.

Honestly, without the Manipulator, "Storm", I don't think I would have learned how to just stand up for myself at some level. I wanna take all the lessons as great, but I think I also learned from the Manipulator about my boundaries and beliefs.

I might've been a little bit more of a pushover if I hadn't really understood the Manipulator in my life. And I still have a tendency to be a bit more on the "wanting to trust and be generous side." But the Manipulator taught me to protect myself before I open up my full trust with people. It's not a bad thing.

When I think of my buddy Kev, the No Nonsense Nurturer, I learned to deepen how to advocate for myself and how to call out shit. To call out the things I think are wrong, and not apologize for it. To not be afraid.

And then with Ify, the Visionary, I learned the idea that you gotta dream big. There's so much out there that needs to be better. If you dream it, it's possible. I couldn't understand what that was without her saying to me, "Ron, at some point in your life, it's not about how much you work, it's the value of the work that you do."

My 47 years of value is what I hope you will see in this book, not the amount of hours I put into it. It's a very "Western widget" way of being able to equate someone's value, "well, how many hours did you work this week?" We don't often look at the value in someone's results.

I'm not saying that you can not work to get value, but at some level, I think we have this overinflated sense that people who work a lot of hours are the ones who have the most value. I don't think that is true.

And then with my wife, the Sage, a lot of what she does is like putting it all together. She gives me the safety to let my hair down fully and be really vulnerable. She's been nudging me for years to learn how to swim. I'm now an adult beginner swimmer at 47.

I still don't know how to drive. I'm your stereotypical native New Yorker. I don't even have a driver's permit so she always has to drive me back after dropping me off. She said to me recently, "you know what would solve this Ron, so I don't have to drop you off? If you would learn how to drive."

Now I have something on my calendar: to study for my permit in June so I can get it to happen and then have my license by fall so I can already drive when we have to start dropping off the girls again to school.

I'm also very cognizant. Like that's an easy drive. It's like a mile away. It's on the streets. I'm not taking the highway or anything crazy.

I can't go it alone. I'm not gonna learn how to swim and learn how to drive and do the things that I've been pushing off because of deep-seated anxiety. I couldn't do it without Shanita saying, "you can do it. It's possible."

I've been really slow on these things. The gift of her supporting me, nurturing me, and being really direct with me is almost like she plays all of these roles of the other six champions sometimes.

There's something about each of these people. I'm just so grateful for the folks who are still alive because of what they continue to bring to my life. Of course, I'm also grateful for the lessons that I've learned from the folks that are no longer in my life or have passed.

These relationships and the journey I've been through are as instructive as what I'm doing today. What I'm doing today is just a tick in the timeline. I'm still "writing more of the book."

There are going to be more people that I continue to add to this list because I wouldn't want people to think that you just need seven. It's a start. You can have more than seven champions. You can have less than seven, in fact, because there are some people that might be able to play multiple roles for you.

You might have these circles of "what you know," "what you know you don't know," and "what you don't know you don't know." When you find enough of these champion archetypes or personality types, the wisdom that they dispense will help fill the "what you don't know you don't know," circle.

Those folks will push you on "what you know you don't know," too. A lot of "what you know" is up to you. I would say that the circle of champions helps you fill out the other 75%.

There's a humility to "I only know so much." I think I know a hell of a lot. But I don't. And when you realize that, then this book will be really helpful.

● ● ● ● ● ● ●

Very, very few of us can jump in the water when we can't swim. Imagine I said, "you know what, I'm going to throw you into the deep end of the pool and your job is to tread water and swim to the other side." Just about everybody would drown.

The best way of doing it alone is to do it in a way where you're supported and taught by the people who want to help you along the way, the people who help you learn how to swim.

Now, have people learned by being thrown off the deep end of the water and swimming? Absolutely. For every person who does well in that, there are many others that don't learn that way. In actuality, learning that way could make them very suspicious of people.

I generally believe in the goodness of people. I wouldn't write this book if I didn't believe in the goodness of people. In every construct, in every culture, there are always people in someone's life who have helped them along the way.

It doesn't always have to be family, doesn't always have to be friends. It could be a stranger you met in the subway. It could be someone you bumped into at Starbucks. It could be someone you met at the gym.

The way that these lessons and these people come into your life bring an understanding, an openness, to the possibilities of how you meet people.

People we need are always around us, but are we willing to see them?

All I did in this book was make it explicit in who I'm seeing. There are probably a hundred people that are not articulated in this book because I didn't go through my

Facebook friends list and my LinkedIn connections list and go, "you know that person? They were really instrumental in my life!"

These are the seven people that first came to mind, but they're not the only.

I almost drowned as a kid. I was with my family on a summer vacation in Orlando. We were in a hotel swimming pool and I was on a floatable Shamu. My brothers pushed me on it and no one was at the deep end of the pool.

I got out. I'm obviously alive. But there's this idea in my head of, "was that the best way for me to learn to be on the Shamu in the deep end of the water?" It would have been better if one of my brothers was side by side with me, knowing I didn't know how to swim. Just to be there and not even push me to that end. It was fun, but there was this assumption that I wouldn't slip off the shamu at the deep end of the pool.

We all slip at some point in our careers. We all need advice at some point. I use that analogy of, "I just don't want people to slip off the shamu at the deep end of the pool."

Now, some people hold on and they're fine. But I think most people don't. You always need someone to hold the shamu, to hold you, to swim with you, to maybe not push you all the way to the deep end.

When people believe that someone has done all of this stuff and gotten wherever they've gotten on their own, that's hardly ever true. And that's not to say that maybe only a handful of people have helped them, right? That might be true. But there's always been someone who's been in their corner who's pushed them.

For Shanita, it's been her grandmother. Her grandmother didn't graduate high school, she only had a fourth grade education. She came from Alabama to work in her uncle's tailoring business. Then she went to Maryland and started her own daycare business for 30 years. What Shanita has learned from her, and I think what I've seen in these patterns of other people's circle of champions, is you don't ever get through life on your own.

There are people that pick you up all the time.

I just want you to think about your life in that way.

Have you ever watched those shows, This Is Your Life? In some ways, Leverage is, in 47 years, a snippet of "This Is Ron's Life."

I want people to realize that you can't go it on your own. This is your life, I can't believe you wouldn't pick out at least three people who impacted you. That you wouldn't bring forth your Empathetic Teacher from fifth grade, your Empathetic Teacher from high school.

I didn't even talk about the man from the Spark office who was very instrumental in helping me when I was going through some shit in high school. I forget John's last name, but John was another Empathetic Teacher. I didn't even talk about him. I start thinking and I realize the abundance of people who have helped me.

I think people are able to thrive when they understand that we're all in this together and people really genuinely want to see you succeed. There's less pressure.

Does that mean there are people that want to take advantage of you and don't want you to succeed? Absolutely. You don't really need to involve those people in your life. You can learn a lesson or you can keep them at arm's distance.

This book is a Love Opus to say, "be conscious and embrace the people that love and care about you personally and professionally."

You'll be where you need to when you do that. You just will. I don't see any other way.

● ● ● ... ● ● ●

Your story fucking matters. Who you are and who you want to be and sharing what you've learned is as valuable as the book that I've written.

I've learned that there's such power in my story. I had someone in my network big-up me and tag me in a LinkedIn post that said, "you should follow someone like Ron because he talks about belonging."

When I share my story, what I want the reader to know is that I always belong and I've always had this tension in my life, believe it or not. I don't always feel like I belong in every situation, every circumstance. There's always this part of me that's never fully belonging.

But with my circle of champions, these people, I 100% belong with them. They're the people I love and care about. These are my people.

I want people to deeply, deeply understand that. That their story fucking matters as much as anybody who writes a book or does a podcast.

There's a certain level of me understanding my mortality in ways, just because of age. There's someone I went to junior high school with who had been dealing with diabetes who I found out passed away recently. I'm at the age where I find a little bit more people in my age group that I've known are dying. It's real.

It's not like, "oh, my God, I'm shocked. Someone died at my age? Why is that?" In my late 40s, it's a little bit more humbling. That starts to be the age where health complications and other things start getting people.

There's a deep gratitude that I want you to know I have for the life that I've lived so far. While I believe that I have much more to go, I know I don't control that.

So what?

Life is sweeter because of the people you work through and with.

Be present.

Love the moment that you're in.

Embrace it. You won't get it back.

About the Author

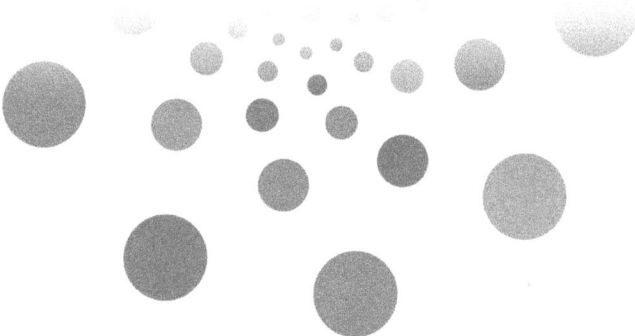

Ron Rapatalo is the seventh child of Philippine immigrants, born and raised in New York City, and a product of New York City public schools.

He was destined to become a doctor, but decided while at NYU that was not what he wanted to do. After meandering through corporate successes, Ron turned towards activism and education, and has now been active in the social impact sector for 20 years. He is currently an Associate Partner at a national talent equity consulting firm focused on social impact organizations.

Ron and his amazing wife are the parents of two beautiful girls, and they live in Jersey City, New Jersey.

He works out fervently and loves to talk smack.

www.ingramcontent.com/pod-product-compliance
Lightning Source LLC
Chambersburg PA
CBHW051435270326
41935CB00019B/1830